A+

Certification™

Core Module

Test Prep Kit

A+ Certification™ Core Module Test Prep Kit

Ted Chandler

IDG Books Worldwide, Inc.
An International Data Group Company
Foster City, CA • Chicago, IL • Indianapolis, IN • New York, NY

A+ Certification ™ Core Module Test Prep Kit

Published by
IDG Books Worldwide, Inc.
An International Data Group Company
919 E. Hillsdale Blvd., Suite 400
Foster City, CA 94404
www.idgbooks.com (IDG Books Worldwide Web site)

Library of Congress Catalog Card Number: 99-66362

ISBN: 0-7645-3302-9

Printed in the United States of America

10 9 8 7 6 5 4 3 2 1

1P/RU/QZ/ZZ/FC

Distributed in the United States by IDG Books Worldwide, Inc.

Distributed by CDG Books Canada Inc. for Canada; by Transworld Publishers Limited in the United Kingdom; by IDG Norge Books for Norway; by IDG Sweden Books for Sweden; by IDG Books Australia Publishing Corporation Pty. Ltd. for Australia and New Zealand; by TransQuest Publishers Pte Ltd. for Singapore, Malaysia, Thailand, Indonesia, and Hong Kong; by Gotop Information Inc. for Taiwan; by ICG Muse, Inc. for Japan; by Norma Comunicaciones S.A. for Colombia; by Intersoft for South Africa; by Eyrolles for France; by International Thomson Publishing for Germany, Austria and Switzerland; by Distribuidora Cuspide for Argentina; by LR International for Brazil; by Galileo Libros for Chile; by Ediciones ZETA S.C.R. Ltda. for Peru; by WS Computer Publishing Corporation, Inc., for the Philippines; by Contemporanea de Ediciones for Venezuela; by Express Computer Distributors for the Caribbean and West Indies; by Micronesia Media Distributor, Inc. for Micronesia; by Grupo Editorial Norma S.A. for Guatemala; by Chips Computadoras S.A. de C.V. for Mexico; by Editorial Norma de Panama S.A. for Panama; by American Bookshops for Finland.

For general information on IDG Books Worldwide's books in the U.S., please call our Consumer Customer Service department at 800-762-2974. For reseller information, including discounts and premium sales, please call our Reseller Customer Service department at 800-434-3422.

For information on where to purchase IDG Books Worldwide's books outside the U.S., please contact our International Sales department at 317-596-5530 or fax 317-596-5692.

For consumer information on foreign language translations, please contact our Customer Service department at 800-434-3422, fax 317-596-5692, or e-mail rights@idgbooks.com.

For information on licensing foreign or domestic rights, please phone +1-650-655-3109.

For sales inquiries and special prices for bulk quantities, please contact our Sales department at 650-655-3200 or write to the address above.

For information on using IDG Books Worldwide's books in the classroom or for ordering examination copies, please contact our Educational Sales department at 800-434-2086 or fax 317-596-5499.

For press review copies, author interviews, or other publicity information, please contact our Public Relations department at 650-655-3000 or fax 650-655-3299.

For authorization to photocopy items for corporate, personal, or educational use, please contact Copyright Clearance Center, 222 Rosewood Drive, Danvers, MA 01923, or fax 978-750-4470.

is a registered trademark or trademark under exclusive license to IDG Books Worldwide, Inc. from International Data Group, Inc. in the United States and/or other countries.

ABOUT IDG BOOKS WORLDWIDE

Welcome to the world of IDG Books Worldwide.

IDG Books Worldwide, Inc., is a subsidiary of International Data Group, the world's largest publisher of computer-related information and the leading global provider of information services on information technology. IDG was founded more than 30 years ago by Patrick J. McGovern and now employs more than 9,000 people worldwide. IDG publishes more than 290 computer publications in over 75 countries. More than 90 million people read one or more IDG publications each month.

Launched in 1990, IDG Books Worldwide is today the #1 publisher of best-selling computer books in the United States. We are proud to have received eight awards from the Computer Press Association in recognition of editorial excellence and three from Computer Currents' First Annual Readers' Choice Awards. Our best-selling ...For Dummies® series has more than 50 million copies in print with translations in 31 languages. IDG Books Worldwide, through a joint venture with IDG's Hi-Tech Beijing, became the first U.S. publisher to publish a computer book in the People's Republic of China. In record time, IDG Books Worldwide has become the first choice for millions of readers around the world who want to learn how to better manage their businesses.

Our mission is simple: Every one of our books is designed to bring extra value and skill-building instructions to the reader. Our books are written by experts who understand and care about our readers. The knowledge base of our editorial staff comes from years of experience in publishing, education, and journalism — experience we use to produce books to carry us into the new millennium. In short, we care about books, so we attract the best people. We devote special attention to details such as audience, interior design, use of icons, and illustrations. And because we use an efficient process of authoring, editing, and desktop publishing our books electronically, we can spend more time ensuring superior content and less time on the technicalities of making books.

You can count on our commitment to deliver high-quality books at competitive prices on topics you want to read about. At IDG Books Worldwide, we continue in the IDG tradition of delivering quality for more than 30 years. You'll find no better book on a subject than one from IDG Books Worldwide.

John Kilcullen
Chairman and CEO
IDG Books Worldwide, Inc.

Steven Berkowitz
President and Publisher
IDG Books Worldwide, Inc.

Eighth Annual Computer Press Awards ≥1992

Ninth Annual Computer Press Awards ≥1993

Tenth Annual Computer Press Awards ≥1994

Eleventh Annual Computer Press Awards ≥1995

Credits

Acquisitions Editor
John Read

Development Editors
Jennifer Rowe
Robert MacSweeney

Technical Editor
Brad Harris

Copy Editor
Lauren Kennedy

Book Designer
Dan Zeigler

Illustrator
Joan Carol

Production
York Graphic Services

Proofreading and Indexing
York Production Services

About the Author

Ted Chandler, professor of engineering, is a full-time CIS instructor at the Cisco Systems Networking Academy at Cuyamaca College near San Diego, California. In addition to teaching the Cisco Certified Network Associate (CCNA) program in the Academy, he teaches courses in A+ certification, Network+ certification, and structured network cabling. Ted has many years of engineering, management, and teaching experience in both the computer industry and education fields. His certifications include A+ Certified Technician and Network+, and he is a registered professional engineer in the state of California.

To the youth and to our Sara,
whose memory inspires me to teach and write.

Preface

Welcome to *A+ Certification Core Module Test Prep Kit!* This book helps you not only pass, but ace the A+ Core Module section of the two-part *A+ Certified Computer Service Technician Examination.* It provides you with essential computer hardware knowledge and valuable exam insights that ensure results — *A+ certification.*

As an A+ certified computer service technician, you will join the fastest growing certification program in the computer industry. Sponsored by the 7,500-member Computing Technology Industry Association (CompTIA), the A+ certification program is an internationally recognized standard for computer service professionals. By testing candidates on PC hardware and operating systems, the program establishes a benchmark level of knowledge and competency expected from entry-level computer service technicians. The A+ credential validates that the holder has reached this level of knowledge and competency, and the credential is both broadly accepted and extremely valued by the computer industry worldwide.

Once you have obtained A+ certification, you have the competitive edge essential for rapidly advancing in the exploding field of information technology. A+ certification also serves as the foundation, or launching pad for computer service professionals who are pursuing other valuable industry certifications, such as the Microsoft Certified Professional (MCP), Cisco Certified Networking Associate (CCNA), and CompTIA's Network+ certification.

About the A+ Certification Exam

To become A+ certified, you must pass the two-part multiple-choice exam: A+ Core Module and A+ DOS/Windows. Each section has 70 questions, and you must score 65 percent on the A+ Core Module and 66 percent on the A+ DOS/Windows as well as pass both exam parts within 90 calendar days of each other to obtain certification.

Part I: A+ Core Module

The A+ Core Module exam tests the candidate's knowledge of and competency in installing, configuring, upgrading, troubleshooting, and repairing computer hardware. It focuses on PC systems, printers, networks, personnel safety, and preventative maintenance, and consists of the following computer technology domains (the approximate number of questions for each category are in parentheses):

- Installation, configuration, and upgrading (21)
- Diagnosing and troubleshooting (14)
- Safety and preventive maintenance (7)
- Motherboards, processors, and memory (8)
- Printers (7)
- Portable systems (3)
- Basic networks (4)
- Customer satisfaction (6)

Although the customer satisfaction questions are scored, the results are for your information only; they are not included in your final pass/fail grade calculation.

Part II: A+ DOS/Windows

The A+ DOS/Windows exam tests the candidate's knowledge of and competency with DOS, Windows 3.x (Windows 3.1 and WFW 3.11), and Windows 95. It consists of the following software technology domains (the approximate number of questions for each category is in parentheses):

- Function, structure, operation, and file management (21)
- Memory management (7)
- Installation, configuration, and upgrading (17)
- Diagnosing and troubleshooting (17)
- Networks (8)

The total number of A+ DOS/Windows exam questions are weighted, with 75 percent for Windows 95 and 25 percent for DOS/Windows 3.*x.*

About the Testing Centers

With more than 700 testing centers worldwide, Sylvan Prometric is the official A+ certification-testing vendor for CompTIA. When you have completed this book and are ready to take and ace either one or both parts of the A+ Certification exam, call Sylvan Prometric for a testing appointment at 1-800-77-MICRO (1-800-776-4276) between 7:00 a.m. and 6:00 p.m. (eastern standard time) Monday through Friday. To register for the A+ Certification exam online, access www.2test.com. Before contacting Sylvan Prometric, be prepared to provide your name, Social Security number, address, and a valid credit card number. The combined cost for both A+ Certification exam parts is $256.

About This Book

A+ Certification Core Module Test Prep Kit is written by an expert to help you ace Part I — A+ Core Module — of the A+ Certification exam. This book closely corresponds to CompTIA's published A+ Core Module exam outline, and it accurately reflects each exam domain, including (the weighted percentage of chapter coverage is in parentheses):

- Installation, configuration, and upgrading (30%)
- Diagnosing and troubleshooting (20%)
- Safety and preventive maintenance (10%)
- Motherboards, processors, and memory (10%)
- Printers (10%)
- Portable systems (5%)
- Basic networks (5%)
- Customer satisfaction (10%)

A+ Certification Core Module Test Prep Kit not only mirrors the topics and material in the actual A+ Core Module exam, but it is also designed and structured to help you use your test preparation time wisely, efficiently, and effectively. This book includes the following highlighted chapter study aids:

- **Official Word** lists the official A+ Certification exam objectives covered in the chapter.
- **Inside Scoop** immediately follows Official Word and gives you the author's insight and expertise about the exam content covered in the chapter.
- **Are You Prepared?** is a chapter pretest that enables you to check your knowledge beforehand. (If you score well on the pretest, you may not need to review the chapter!) The chapter pretest helps you focus your study; answers with cross-references to chapter information immediately follow the questions, helping you further target your review.
- **Have You Mastered?** is a chapter post-test of ten multiple-choice questions followed by answers, analysis, and cross-references to the chapter discussion. The questions help you check your progress and pinpoint what you've learned and what you still need to study.

Within each chapter, icons call your attention to the following features:

Test Tips are hints and strategies for passing the exam and help strengthen your test-taking skills.

Test Traps warn you of pitfalls and loopholes you're likely to see in actual exam questions.

Pop Quizzes offer instant testing of hot exam topics.

Know This provides a quick summary of essential elements of topics you *will* see on the exam.

At the back of the book, you'll find a full-length practice exam. It is multiple choice and has questions and answer selections that mimic the certification exam's style, number of questions, and content to give you the closest experience to the real thing. An answer key and a detailed analysis of why the correct answers are right, and why the distracters are wrong follow the practice exam.

Acknowledgments

I have nothing but kind words for the IDG Books team; they have helped me get through the daunting task of writing not only my first book, but writing two books virtually simultaneously. Special thanks to my lead development editor, Jennifer Rowe, for her many insightful comments and continued encouragement; to development editors Bob MacSweeney, for helping shape several chapters, and Matt Lusher, for his contributions to Chapter 1. Thank you also to my copy editor, Lauren Kennedy, for her keen eye, and to my technical editor, Brad Harris, for a thorough review.

I appreciate the comments and guidance; I now understand the whole editorial process and am ready to take on the next book!

And finally, a special, heartfelt thanks to my wife, Mary Kay, for always being my best friend in good times and in bad.

Contents at a Glance

Contents

9 Input and Output Peripheral Devices 201

12 Total Customer Satisfaction 269

Computer
Hardware
Overview

THIS CHAPTER PROVIDES an overview of the hardware devices that make up the microcomputer system. It prepares you for A+ Core exam questions on the primary terms, concepts, and functions of computer system modules, field replaceable units (FRUs), and discrete electrical and mechanical components. This chapter also prepares you for questions on classifying system modules and FRUs by primary computing process functions such as input, process, storage, and output.

Exam Material in This Chapter

Based on Objectives

- Identify basic terms, concepts, and functions of system modules and field replaceable units
- Classify modules and units by computing process functions
- Know how modules and units work

Based on Author's Experience

- Know how to define a microcomputer system
- Learn which core and peripheral devices make up a microcomputer system
- Anticipate questions concerning the various terms, acronyms, and functions of system modules and FRUs
- Understand how system modules and FRUs are classified: input, process, storage, and output (also referred to as IPSO)
- Expect questions regarding how system modules and FRUs work during normal operation
- Know the functions of discrete electrical and mechanical components, such as integrated circuits, resistors, capacitors, transistors, diodes, jumpers, and switches

Are You Prepared?

Test your knowledge with the following questions. Then you'll know if you're prepared for the material in this chapter or if you should review problem areas.

1. **Which of the following components are considered to be FRUs? (Choose all that apply.)**

   ☐ A. System boards
   ☐ B. System clocks
   ☐ C. Power supplies
   ☐ D. Monitors

2. **What is the primary function of a capacitor in an electrical circuit?**

   ☐ A. Switch a signal
   ☐ B. Amplify a signal
   ☐ C. Retain an electrical charge
   ☐ D. Transform analog-to-digital signals

3. **Which of the following is considered a system input device?**

   ☐ A. RAM
   ☐ B. ROM
   ☐ C. Hard disk drive
   ☐ D. Monitors

Answers:

1. A, C, and D

   System boards, power supplies, and monitors are classified as FRUs because they can be easily replaced in the field without using special tools or equipment (such as a soldering gun). System clocks, on the other hand, are not classified as FRUs because they are timing circuits incorporated in the chip set on the system board and cannot be easily replaced. See the "Identifying FRUs Inside the System Unit Case" section.

2. C

   Capacitors retain electrical charges and release them gradually over time whereas transistors switch and amplify signals, and analog-to-digital converters perform analog-to-digital signal transformation functions.

   Small capacitors are often used on system boards to protect chips from over-voltage spikes. Large capacitors are used in power supplies and cathode-ray tubes (CRTs) as primary electrical storage devices. See the "Understanding Printed Circuit Boards" section.

3. B

   Read-only memory (ROM) is an input device. Random-access memory (RAM) and hard disk drives are data storage devices, and a monitor is an output device. See the "Defining System Modules and Functions" section.

Defining Microcomputer Systems

More than any other machine, computers symbolize the significant technological advancements made over the past 50 years. First-generation computers, introduced in the early 1950s, were based on vacuum tubes. In second-generation computers, which appeared in the early 1960s, transistors replaced vacuum tubes, and, in third-generation computers, integrated circuits replaced discrete transistors. In the mid-1970s, large-scale integration (LSI) component designs appeared, enabling thousands of circuits to be incorporated into a single chip. (It is the microprocessor — the brain of the computer — that incorporates LSI.) The personal computer (PC), a computer designed to be used by one person at a time, is an example of a fourth-generation computer. And currently, fifth-generation computers incorporate very-large-scale integration (VLSI) chip design, which offers sophisticated approaches to computing, such as super-miniaturization and artificial intelligence.

Computer Classifications

Computers are classified according to speed, size, cost, and capability. Also, computers are generally grouped as follows:

- Supercomputers
- Mainframes
- Minicomputers
- Super Minicomputers
- Workstations
- Microcomputers

Microcomputers are computers built around a single-chip microprocessor. Although originally less powerful than minicomputers and mainframes, microcomputers have evolved into powerful machines capable of complex tasks. The power of today's microcomputers, or PCs, rival mainframes built just a few years ago, at a fraction of the cost.

Together with *read-only memory* (RAM), the microprocessor, or *central processing unit* (CPU), forms the core of the microcomputer. All other devices that make up the PC support these two integrated components.

A basic PC system is composed of a system unit case, keyboard, mouse, and monitor; and multimedia PCs add sound, video, and CD-ROM capability to a basic system.

A+ Core exam questions focus on multimedia PCs with the latest Pentium processors and advanced peripheral devices, including printers and modems.

The software that runs the computer's hardware is known as system software or the computer's *operating system* (OS). Application software, on the other hand, enables PC users to perform specific tasks, such as word processing, financial analysis, and data base management.

When you answer A+ Core exam questions, remember that hardware can be seen and touched; software cannot because it does not have a physical form. Many PC components contain both hardware and software.

Defining System Modules and Functions

Computer hardware and software systems incorporate *modular designs*, which means that the system is broken down into smaller units or modules. Each module is designed, developed, and tested independently before the final system is assembled. Modules are also designed to perform a particular task or function, and then they become part of a library of task-oriented modules that may possibly be reused for other similar computer system designs.

Modular printed circuit boards also support the computer design concept, *open architecture*. With this concept, circuit boards and adapter cards can be installed in expansion slots on the system board to either expand or customize a computer system. Open architecture requires published specifications to ensure common modular designs and functionality throughout the computer industry.

The Functional Classifications of System Modules

Computer system modules are functionally classified as follows:

- Input
- Processing
- Storage
- Output

Figure 1-1 presents a computer system block diagram. It graphically illustrates primary computer system modules and relationships among the modules. Arrows designate the relationships and provide clues about the system process function of a given module. For example, the keyboard, mouse, and ROM modules provide data input functions to the processor, while the processor and RAM modules perform integrated data processing and short-term memory functions. Disk drive modules furnish long-term data and perform information storage functions, and the monitor screen and print modules contribute information output functions to the computer system.

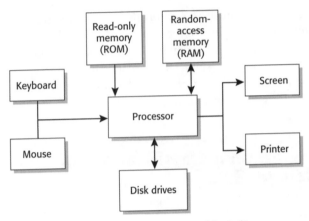

Figure 1-1 *A microcomputer system block diagram*

Learn the acronym IPSO, which is formed from input, processing, storage, and output. Then memorize the function of each primary module using the block diagram for reference and employ IPSO as a memory jog during the A+ Core exam.

Identifying FRUs Inside the System Unit Case

Field replaceable units (FRUs) are devices that can be easily replaced without special tools and equipment, such as a soldering gun or multimeter. The most obvious and most visible replaceable modules, which are also *classified* as FRUs, in a PC include the system unit case, monitor, printer, keyboard, and mouse. But many of the components and circuit boards inside the system unit case can also be easily replaced.

The system unit case is the sheet metal cabinet that houses the main components and circuit boards of the computer system. The tower, desktop, and portable system unit case styles are the most popular.

The FRUs inside the tower system unit case (see Figure 1-2) are often the same as those inside the desktop case (see Figure 1-3), except that, naturally, each case's FRUs are located and configured differently to fit their respective case style or form factor.

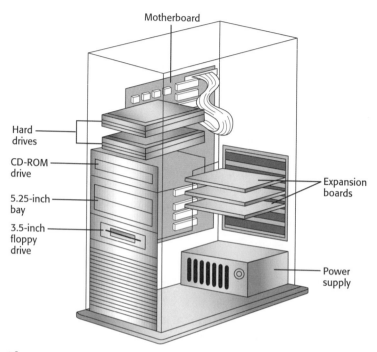

Figure 1-2 *FRUs inside a typical tower system unit case*

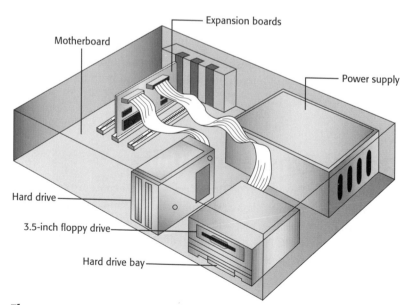

Figure 1-3 *FRUs inside a typical desktop system unit case*

System Boards

A system board (also called the *motherboard, main board,* or *planar board*) is the most important FRU in the system unit case. As the foundation of the computer system, the system board is the main circuit board and contains such primary components as the central processing unit (CPU), RAM, the read-only memory basic input/output system (ROM BIOS), buses, the chip set, and expansion slots.

A system board is categorized by its form factor — its size, shape, design, and component layout. Current system board form factors include the ATX (Advanced Technology X), Baby AT, and Full AT. System boards that incorporate the ATX form factor are the most popular in today's PC marketplace.

System Board Form Factors

A system board is categorized by its form factor — its size, shape, design, and component layout. Current system boards incorporate the following form factors:

- ATX
- Baby AT
- Full AT

A+ Core exam questions use the terms motherboard and system board interchangeably. Know that both terms refer to the same FRU.

Central Processing Units

The central processing unit (CPU) interprets and executes program instructions, and transfers data and information among the other system devices and resources. Together with the RAM, the CPU constitutes the core of the computer. CPUs are generally rated by a millions of cycles per second (MHz) clock speed. CPUs are mounted in sockets or slots, enabling them to be easily removed and replaced without special tools or equipment.

Random-Access Memory

Random-access memory (RAM) is the short-term, volatile memory that the CPU uses to store and retrieve data, calculation results, and program instructions. RAM also stores data for other hardware devices, such as video adapters and sound cards. All binary data in RAM is deleted entirely when the computer is turned off. RAM is mounted in memory banks on the system board and can be easily replaced without special tools or equipment.

True or False?

1. The three current system board form factors are Full AT, Baby AT, and ATX.
2. The acronym FRU means functionally repairable unit.
3. The keyboard is an input device.

Answers: *1. True   2. False   3. True*

Read-only Memory Basic Input/Output System

Read-only memory (ROM) is long-term, non-volatile memory that per-manently stores the BIOS. The BIOS is the software that runs a power-on self-test (POST), initiates loading the operating system into RAM, runs the System Setup program, and facilitates communication between the CPU and system hardware devices. ROM BIOS is also called *firmware*.

ROM BIOS Functions

ROM BIOS (also called firmware) has these functions:

- Runs POST
- Initiates loading the operating system
- Runs the System Setup program
- Facilitates communication between the CPU and hardware devices

You should know for the exam that one beep during computer boot (startup) indicates that POST has not found any errors during its functional check of the basic system devices. You should also recognize that the System Setup program provides access to the Complementary Metal-Oxide Semiconductor (CMOS). The CMOS, which stores hardware device configuration settings, is located on the battery-powered real-time clock (RTC) chip.

A+ Core exam questions ask about both RAM and ROM. Be sure you know the differences between the two and do not become confused by their acronyms. Remember that RAM is volatile, short-term data storage or memory, whereas ROM is non-volatile, long-term data storage.

Hard Disk Drives

The hard disk drive (HDD) is an electromechanical, long-term data storage device that contains from two to eight rigid disks (also called *platters*) that are coated with a thin film of magnetically sensitive material. The platters are assembled on a spindle (shaft), and a spindle motor rotates the assembly at high speeds. Read/write heads record and retrieve binary data by sensing or changing the magnetic field polarity of the platter's surface material. The HDD is often referred to as the computer's fixed disk, and the operating system designates the HDD as drive C.

Floppy Disk Drives

The floppy disk drive (FDD) is similar in design concept and long-term data storage function to the HDD, except that the FDD contains a single flexible magnetic disk that is easy to remove. It also holds far less data than the HDD. The operating system designates the FDD as either drive A or drive B, depending on the FDD setting in the CMOS.

Compact Disc, Read-only Memory Drives

The compact disc, read-only memory (CD-ROM) drive stores digital information on removable plastic compact discs that are read by laser optics rather than by magnetic means. Compact discs can store up to 650MB (megabytes). The digital data storage capacity of compact discs is far greater than that of floppy disks, but it is not as great as that of current hard disk storage devices.

Power Supplies

Power supplies transform and reduce 110-117 volt (220-230 volt, European power) Alternating Current (AC) line voltages from wall outlets into low-level Direct Current (DC) voltages that are used to power various computer components. Power supplies typically provide + 5 volts and − 5 volts to power FRUs, discrete electrical components on the system board, and peripheral hardware devices. Power supplies also provide + 12 volts and − 12 volts to power disk drives and other motor-driven devices. New ATX power supplies also supply + 3.3 volts to power the latest processors.

Instead of being tested by the POST, power supplies generally use a self-test circuit to check operational readiness during computer boot. A Power_Good signal indicates that there are no problems with the power supply and that it is ready to supply power to the various hardware devices.

Power Supply Voltages and Power_Good Signal

Power supplies provide the following DC voltages:

- + 5 volts
- - 5 volts
- + 12 volts
- - 12 volts
- + 3.3 volts (ATX power supplies)

You should also know that power supplies check their own operational readiness during a computer boot instead of relying on the POST. A Power_Good signal indicates that there is no problem with the power supply.

Video Adapter Cards

Video adapter cards are circuit boards that translate output instructions from the CPU into data that can be displayed on the monitor screen. They are installed in the expansion slots located on the system board, and the video signals are transmitted through a cable, between the system unit case's back panel and the monitor. Video adapter cards contain specialized on-board memory to speed up the complex calculations that render graphics and perform other graphics functions.

Video Adapter Cards

Most new, non-server-type PCs complete the microcomputer system with a video adapter card because it is an essential part of the display subsystem. All other expansion boards and adapter cards are optional.

Modems

Modems (a contraction of MOdulator/DEModulator) translate computer digital signals into analog signals so data may be transmitted over telephone lines, and they translate analog signals into digital signals so that data may be received. Modems can be configured either as an internal circuit card installed in an expansion slot on the system board or as an external device connected to a serial port on the system unit case's back panel. And two methods of reciprocal handshake line pairs are generally available to modems using the RS-232 serial ports:

- DTR/DSR (Data Terminal Ready/Data Set Ready)
- RTS/CTS (Request to Send/Clear to Send)

TEST TRAP Several A+ Core exam questions are on modem attention (AT) commands and communications flow-control. The answers are confusing because there are numerous letter assignments. At the minimum, memorize DTR/DSR and RTS/CTS for reciprocal handshake line pair questions.

Sound Cards

Sound cards are expansion circuit boards that, together with a speaker and a microphone, playback and record sounds using various files and media, such as Windows sound waveform files (WAV) or Musical Instrument Digital Interface (MIDI) files, and compact discs. Sound card designs use either FM Frequency Modulation (FM) synthesizers or wave table files that contain samples of musical instruments.

Network Interface Cards

Network Interface Cards (NICs) connect the computer to local area networks (LANs). NICs are installed in expansion slots on the system board and provide two types of connections for cables linking the computer with the Ethernet LAN:

- RJ-45 connectors are used to connect to twisted-pair cabling
- BNC (Bayonet Naur Connector) connectors are used to connect coaxial cabling

True or False?

1. ROM BIOS contains the POST.

2. RAM is short-term, volatile data storage.

3. Power supplies provide + 9 volts to the system board.

Answers: *1. True   2. True   3. False*

Understanding Printed Circuit Boards

Computers, appliances, instruments, and most other modern electronic devices are made up of printed circuit boards (PCBs). A PCB is a flat piece of epoxy insulating material, on which electrical components are mounted and connected together using thin copper traces to form electrical circuits. The circuits can be on one or on both sides of the board. The discrete components mounted on printed circuit boards include integrated circuits (also known as *ICs* or *chips*), resistors, capacitors, transistors, diodes, switches, jumpers, and connectors. Table 1-1 summarizes the electrical and mechanical components that are generally mounted on a typical printed circuit board.

Several A+ Core exam questions are on discrete electrical and mechanical components mounted on PCBs, such as capacitors, transistors, resistors, and switches. It is important to learn the functions of all the devices presented in Table 1-1.

TABLE 1-1 Typical Printed Circuit Board Components

Component	Description	Illustration
Dual in-line package (DIP) integrated circuits	Specifically designed for circuit board mounting, the DIP is a ceramic or plastic rectangular housing with two rows of protruding edge pins. It contains integrated circuits (ICs), which are micro-miniature electronic circuits etched on silicon wafers.	
Pin grid array (PGA) integrated circuits	Also designed for mounting on circuit boards, the PGA packaged IC has many pins protruding from the bottom surface of the chip. This packaging method is preferred for today's multi-pin IC designs.	
Transistors	A transistor is a solid-state circuit component in which a voltage or a current controls the flow of another current. It can function as an amplifier, a switch, and an oscillator.	
Resistors	A resistor is a circuit component that provides a specific amount resistance (measured in ohms) to current flow. The colored bands indicate the resistance in ohms.	

Continued

TABLE 1-1 *continued*

Component	Description	Illustration
Capacitors	A capacitor is a circuit component that stores a known amount of capacitance (measured in farads), which is the capability to store an electric charge. A capacitor blocks direct current and passes alternating current.	
Diodes	A diode is a circuit component that passes current in one direction only. It is often used to protect ICs from over-voltages and current-reversals.	
DIP switches	A dual in-line package (DIP) switch is a series of small rocker or sliding switches contained by a plastic or ceramic housing.	
Jumpers	A jumper is a small plug or wire that can be connected between two different points in an electrical circuit to alter the circuit path.	

Have You Mastered?

Now it's time to review the concepts in this chapter and apply your knowledge. These questions test your mastery of the material covered in this chapter.

1. What type of memory stores the BIOS?

- ☐ A. RAM
- ☐ B. ROM
- ☐ C. Cache RAM
- ☐ D. Dynamic RAM

The correct answer is **B.** ROM is the physical form of the ROM BIOS chip, and the BIOS software is encoded into the ROM. Refer to the "Identifying FRUs Inside the System Unit Case" section for more information.

2. What does the CMOS contain?

- ☐ A. BIOS
- ☐ B. Complementary Metal-Oxide Semiconductor
- ☐ C. Operating system boot program
- ☐ D. Hardware device configuration settings

The correct answer is **D.** Hardware device configuration settings are stored in the CMOS on the battery-powered RTC chip. Refer to the "Identifying FRUs Inside the System Unit Case" section for more information.

3. What does the acronym FRU mean?

☐ A. Field repairable unit
☐ B. Field replaceable unit
☐ C. Functionally repairable unit
☐ D. Functionally replaceable unit

The correct answer is **B.** Field replaceable units are system modules and components that can be easily replaced in the field without special tools and equipment, such as soldering guns. Refer to the "Identifying FRUs Inside the System Unit Case" section for more information.

4. CPUs work with which component to form the core of the computer?

☐ A. Cache RAM
☐ B. RAM
☐ C. BIOS
☐ D. CMOS

The correct answer is **B.** CPU and RAM comprise the core of the computer. All other devices that make up the computer support these two integrated components. Refer to the "Identifying FRUs Inside the System Unit Case" section for more information.

5. AT class power supplies provide which of the following voltage(s)?

☐ A. 117 volts DC
☐ B. 117 volts AC
☐ C. -5 volts DC
☐ D. 12 volts DC

Both **C** and **D** are correct. Advanced Technology (AT) power supplies provide +/- 5 volts and +/- 12 volts. Refer to the "Identifying FRUs Inside the System Unit Case" section for more information.

6. Which of the following specifications is used to rate CPUs?

☐ A. Amperes
☐ B. Real-time clock speed
☐ C. Watts
☐ D. Clock speed

The correct answer is **D.** CPUs are generally rated by clock speed in millions of cycles per second (MHz). Refer to the "Identifying FRUs Inside the System Unit Case" section for more information.

7. RAM is what type of memory or data storage device? (Choose all that apply.)

☐ A. Volatile
☐ B. Non-volatile
☐ C. Short-term
☐ D. Long-term

Both **A** and **C** are correct. RAM is a volatile, short-term type of memory, whereas ROM is a non-volatile, long-term type of memory. Refer to the "Identifying FRUs Inside the System Unit Case" section for more information.

8. The BIOS performs the following functions during boot: (Choose all that apply.)

☐ A. Tests hardware devices
☐ B. Starts application software
☐ C. Begins loading the operating system
☐ D. Starts the CMOS

Both **A** and **C** are correct. During the boot process, BIOS tests the system hardware devices and starts the operating system loading process. Refer to the "Identifying FRUs Inside the System Unit Case" section for more information.

9. What is the engineering unit measurement for capacitors?

☐ A. Volts
☐ B. Amps
☐ C. Ohms
☐ D. Farads

The correct answer is **D.** Capacitors are measured in farads. Refer to Table 1-1, "Typical Printed Circuit Board Components," for more information.

10. What does a single beep during boot mean?

☐ A. CONFIG.SYS is not loading device drivers.
☐ B. The POST has not discovered any hardware errors.
☐ C. The keyboard is not attached to the system.
☐ D. The File Allocation Table is incorrect.

The correct answer is **B.** A single beep indicates that no errors were found. Refer to the "Identifying FRUs Inside the System Unit Case" section for more information.

Computer
Hardware
Servicing
Basics

THIS CHAPTER EXPLORES the basics of computer hardware servicing. It prepares you for A+ Core exam questions on proper safety and maintenance practices, such as personnel safety, electrostatic discharge (ESD), break/fix servicing concepts, and troubleshooting. This chapter also prepares you for questions regarding precautions to take and proper procedures to follow when disassembling and reassembling the system unit case.

Exam Material in This Chapter

Based on Objectives

- Know proper safety procedures and ESD protection
- Know how to install, configure, and upgrade microcomputer system modules and units
- Know how to troubleshoot and diagnose microcomputer problems

Based on Author's Experience

- Expect questions on how to protect personnel from electrical shock and laser beams
- Be prepared to answer questions on protecting computer components from ESD hazards
- Understand break/fix computer servicing concepts
- Learn basic precautions and proper servicing practices when disassembling and reassembling the system unit case
- Be able to identify basic tools and cleaning supplies required for servicing
- Anticipate several questions regarding error codes and problem text messages

Are You Prepared?

Test your knowledge with the following questions. Then you'll know if you're prepared for the material in this chapter or if you should review problem areas.

1. You should wear an anti-static wrist strap *except* when working on the:

☐ A. CPU (central processing unit)
☐ B. RAM (random-access memory)
☐ C. Video adapter card
☐ D. Monitor

2. When cleaning adapter boards, the first step is to:

☐ A. Lightly tap the boards to remove debris
☐ B. Blow dust away
☐ C. Sponge off dust with a solution of de-mineralized water and detergent
☐ D. Reseat socket devices

3. The term ESD means:

☐ A. Electromagnetic safety discharge
☐ B. Enhanced switching device
☐ C. Electrostatic discharge
☐ D. Electromagnetic surge device

Answers:

1. D *A monitor can generate a voltage potential of 25,000 volts or more while operating. Even after it is turned off, the monitor can still retain high voltages. An anti-static wrist strap helps conduct potentially fatal currents through your body to ground. The other components operate at 5 volts or less and do not store residual voltage. See the "Protecting Service Personnel from Electrical Shock and Laser Beams" section.*

2. D *Reseat the socket devices first because whether you brush or blow the dust away, particles of dust may settle on the connectors; when you then reseat the socket devices, an inadequate connection may occur. See the "Disassembling the System Unit Case" section.*

3. C *Electrostatic electricity is a voltage potential that builds up between objects made of materials that have dissimilar electrical potentials. Discharge occurs when the voltage potential reaches a sufficiently high level. The other answers have no meaning. See the "Protecting Equipment from Electrostatic Discharge " section.*

Protecting Service Personnel from Electrical Shock and Laser Beams

Safety is a major concern when you work on computer systems because high voltage devices are present. Extremely serious shock hazards, with potentially fatal results, exist. For some people, even a small amount of current can cause a cardiac arrest. One way to maintain a safe environment is to be sure personnel are aware of which devices in the computer system produce high voltages and are potentially dangerous. Service personnel should also protect themselves by strictly following safety rules.

The monitor, power supply, and laser printer are three devices with high voltage potential. Laser printers and CD-ROM drives can cause eye injuries because they contain a low-power laser beam.

Monitors

Most monitors produce voltages exceeding 25,000 volts. Even after a monitor is shut off, high residual voltages can be stored in large capacitors or built up on the anode in the cathode-ray tube (CRT). Only a qualified repair technician who knows how to properly discharge the CRT's anode should repair monitors. Figure 2-1 shows a manufacturer's warning label, signaling the extreme danger presented by the CRT inside the monitor housing.

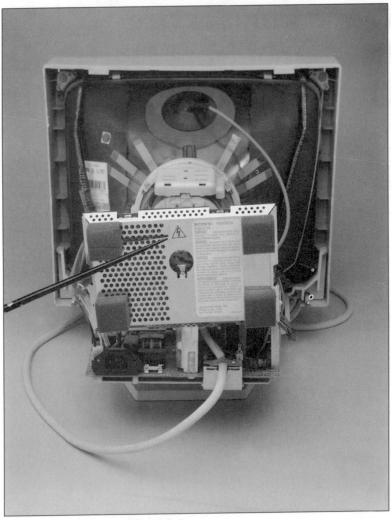

Figure 2-1 *A CRT warning label*

Power Supplies

As with monitors, residual voltages can be stored in large capacitors in the power supply, even after the computer has been turned off. To avoid hazards, it is best to replace a failed power supply rather than disassemble and fix it. If you decide to repair a power supply, ensure that the power cable is disconnected from the wall outlet. Figure 2-2 is a manufacturer's electrical hazard warning label on a power supply.

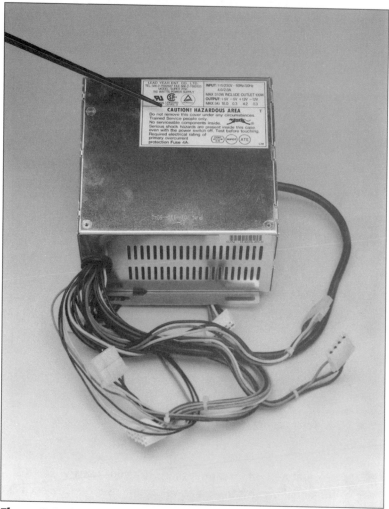

Figure 2-2 *A power supply warning label*

Laser Printers

Always use extreme caution when working on laser printers. Although a laser beam is invisible and may contain only several milliwatts (mW) of power, looking directly at the beam can cause serious eye injury. Laser printers also have the potential for electrical shocks because of the high voltages (up to 2000 volts) generated in their power supply subsystem. Figure 2-3 shows where the electrical and laser beam warning label on a laser printer is located.

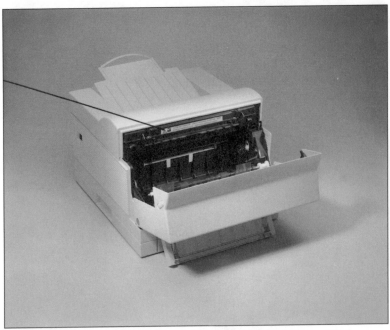

Figure 2-3 *A laser printer electrical and laser beam warning label*

 Several A+ Core exam questions test your knowledge on potential hazards from high-voltage or laser devices, such as monitors, power supplies, laser printers, and CD-ROM drives. Specifically, remember that monitors generate up to 25,000 volts, and that you should never wear an anti-static ground strap when servicing a monitor.

Personnel Safety Rules

To prevent potential electrical shock and laser beam injuries, follow these personnel safety rules:

- Have a qualified technician repair CRTs.
- Never service a monitor while wearing an anti-static wrist strap.
- Disconnect all cables prior to servicing a monitor.
- Never look directly at a laser beam.
- Never work on equipment while standing on a wet or damp floor.
- Never work on a metal workbench top without a grounded rubber mat.
- Never work on equipment while wearing jewelry.
- Always shut off the power at the power switch, but keep the power cord in the wall outlet prior to removing the system unit cover.
- Never work on the power supply with the power cable connected to the wall outlet.
- Consider replacing the power supply rather than repairing it.

 The discrete components inside the power supply and monitor that store high voltages are capacitors — not resistors, transistors, rectifiers, or diodes.

Protecting Equipment from Electrostatic Discharge

Electrostatic discharge (ESD) is also a major concern when working on a computer. In fact, it is the primary cause of computer component failures when they are shipped, stored, handled, or installed.

ESD occurs when static electricity builds up between two objects made from materials with dissimilar electrical potentials. It then discharges when the voltage potential reaches a sufficiently high level or discharge threshold. ESD does not harm humans, but it does pose a significant threat to electronic equipment and discrete components. Integrated circuits (ICs) or chips, which are manufactured using Complementary Metal-Oxide Semiconductor (CMOS) technology, are especially susceptible to damage from electrostatic discharge. An overvoltage of only 10 volts may damage some chips and static electricity in the human body has the potential to build up to 10,000 volts. Therefore, appropriate ESD protection, such as wearing an anti-static wrist strap and working on a grounded rubber mat, must be established. If an anti-static wrist strap is not available, an alternative ESD precaution is to touch the fan guard or another unpainted surface on the back panel before touching any component inside the system unit case. Figure 2-4 demonstrates using an anti-static wrist strap and a grounded work mat to protect the electronic components and circuits on the circuit cards.

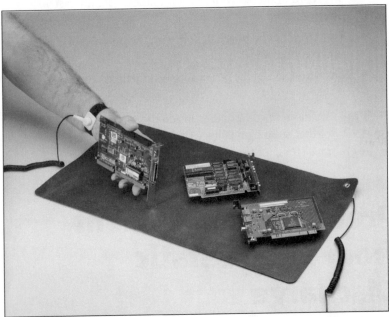

Figure 2-4 *Using an anti-static wrist strap and grounded work mat*

True or False?

1. CRTs can contain up to 25,000 volts, which is very dangerous to humans.

2. The human body can build up to 10,000 volts of static electricity, which is not dangerous to humans but is deadly to CMOS chips.

3. Electrostatic discharge occurs between objects made from materials of dissimilar electrical potentials.

Answers: *1. True   2. True   3. True*

Work Area Electrostatic Discharge Protection

The following recommendations will help prevent ESD-related damage to equipment in the work area:

- Keep the humidity above 50 percent by using a humidifier.
- Use grounded rubber mats on the workbench tops.
- Use grounded or rubber floor mats in work areas.
- Ensure that the storage shelves are lined with anti-static material.
- Use an anti-static spray on the carpets and work areas.
- Post ESD hazard signs.

ESD Potential

Low humidity is caused by relatively low moisture content in the atmosphere. This condition creates high ESD potential. High humidity creates low ESD potential. For the A+ Core exam, remember the following two contrasts:

- Low humidity = high ESD potential
- High humidity = low ESD potential

Personnel Electrostatic Discharge Protection

To prevent ESD-related damage to equipment, service personnel should adhere to the following guidelines:

- Always wear an anti-static wrist strap *except* while servicing the CRTs.

- Touch the fan guard or another unpainted surface on the back panel before touching any component inside the system unit case.

- While working inside the system unit case, periodically touch an unpainted surface.

- Always handle circuit boards by gripping their edges.

- Never touch the circuit traces or the discrete electronic parts and connectors on a circuit board.

KNOW THIS ESD Risk and Prevention

You should know the following key points regarding ESD:

- An over-voltage of only 10 volts can cause a component to fail.

- Greatest ESD risk occurs when atmospheric humidity is *below* 50 percent or has a low moisture content.

- Even though a human may not feel a buildup of electrostatic electricity, it can be deadly to discrete electronic components — even when they are installed on a circuit board.

- Always wear an anti-static wrist strap *except* while working on CRTs.

- Check the resistance (> 1 Megaohm) of the wrist strap periodically using an ohmmeter to ensure that it remains functional.

Assembling a Basic Servicing Tool Kit

Most computer servicing can be accomplished with a basic tool kit. For example, a computer service tool kit might consist of nut drivers; straight-slot, Phillips-head, and Torx-head screwdrivers; a chip extraction tool; a can of compressed air; cleaning brushes; a bottle of mild detergent and water solution; lint-free clothes; a loop-back connector; an anti-static wrist strap; and a vacuum cleaner.

It is best to use a lint-free damp cloth and a mild detergent when cleaning the plastic external surfaces of the monitor, system unit case, and keyboard. Compressed air or a vacuum cleaner removes dust and dirt from printed circuit boards, keyboards, and does not build up static electricity, but a vacuum cleaner disperses less dirt and dust.

Figure 2-5 shows the contents of a computer servicing tool kit.

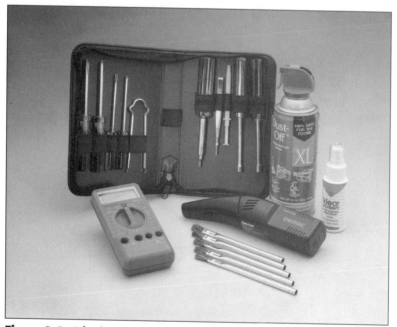

Figure 2-5 *A basic computer servicing tool kit*

A multimeter should also be included in a service tool kit. Standard multimeters are instruments that measure alternating current (AC) and direct current (DC), including the voltage (volts), amperage (amps), and resistance (ohms). They are indispensable for diagnosing electrical problems. For example, checking the condition of a fuse can be performed using the ohmmeter in any range to measure the fuse's resistance. If the resistance is less than one ohm, the fuse is still good. If the resistance is infinite, the fuse is bad (or *blown*).

 Do not be fooled into working out Ohm's law when answering the A+ Core exam question regarding the resistance of a good fuse. The answer is simple: A blown fuse has infinite resistance, whereas a good fuse will approach zero resistance.

It is also common to use the multimeter to check the power supply input and output voltages. Note that when measuring nominal 117 volts AC wall-outlet voltage, which is the input voltage to the power supply, the AC voltage range on the multimeter must be set at the 200 volts range. Additionally, note that a 10 percent tolerance is acceptable when measuring the DC power supply output voltages to the system board and motor-driven devices.

A loopback connector is another useful troubleshooting tool. It is used to diagnose serial and parallel port problems by directing data between the port connector's output and input pins.

General Computer Servicing

You should know the following key points regarding general computer servicing:

- A functional fuse's resistance is less than one ohm.

- The AC voltmeter section of the multimeter is set to 200 volts to read nominal 117 volts AC line voltage from the wall outlet.

- A 10 percent tolerance is acceptable when measuring power supply voltage output.

- A loopback connector directs data between the I/O port connector's output and input pins.

- A lint-free cloth and a mild solution of detergent and water should be used to clean external plastic surfaces of the computer.

- Compressed air is generally used to remove dust and dirt from printed circuit boards and power supplies.

Defining Computer Module Servicing

The system modules and field replaceable units (FRUs) that compose a computer system contain thousands of discrete electronic and mechanical components and hundreds of electrical circuits mounted on printed circuit boards (PCBs). Fixing or replacing an individual component or repairing a circuit is not only impractical but it is also likely to be impossible. Additionally, modules and FRUs often cost less to replace than to repair. The best practice when servicing computers is to focus on module and FRU maintenance, rather than on fixing individual parts or circuit boards. The approach to servicing computer modules is as follows:

1. Isolate the problem as either a hardware or a software module problem

2. Determine why the module or the FRU malfunctioned

3. Make simple changes to correct the problem

4. Replace the faulty module or FRU if necessary

5. Test to ensure that the problem has been corrected

True or False?

1. A blown fuse has zero resistance.

2. The resistance of a wrist strap should be > 1 Megaohm.

3. The greatest ESD risk occurs when the atmospheric humidity is high.

Answers: *1. False   2. True   3. False*

Identifying Error Codes and Problem Messages

Error codes and problem text messages play an important role in diagnosing computer problems. They are usually displayed on the screen or during computer boot. Most hardware error codes are generated by the basic input/output system (BIOS) or the operating system (OS) and often occur during the power-on self-test (POST). Although each BIOS manufacturer has a unique set of error codes, most common error codes for IBM PC-compatible computers fall under the following general numeric categories:

100 series	System board
200 series	RAM
300 series	Keyboard
500 series	Color graphics adapter (CGA)
600 series	Floppy disk controller
900 series	Parallel port I/O communications
1100 series	Serial port I/O communications
1700 series	Hard disk controller

2400 series	Video graphics adapter (VGA)
3900 series	Professional graphics adapter (PGA)
C600 and C700	ROM BIOS

Computer problems also are evident by the following on-screen text error messages:

- **Parity Check 1** indicates problems with the RAM.
- **Parity Check 2** indicates a problem with the RAM.
- **Error Code 201** indicates a problem with the RAM.
- **GPF** (General Protection Fault) is a Windows 3.*x* error message that indicates that an application has made an unauthorized attempt to access RAM or that memory management commands are improperly set. Rebooting the computer often solves the problem.
- **Fatal Exception Error** is a Windows 95 error message indicating a problem with device drivers stored in RAM. Rebooting the computer often solves the problem.

Parity Error

Parity error messages always indicate a problem with RAM; typically, the data output from the RAM does not match the input.

Disassembling the System Unit Case

Before removing the cover from the system unit case, ensure that it is necessary to do so and review the rules for personnel safety and ESD hazard protection. Once you do this, remove the cover from the system unit. Figure 2-6 illustrates removing the cover from a tower system unit case. Figure 2-7 depicts removing the cover from a desktop system unit case.

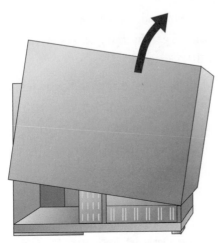

Figure 2-6 *Removing the cover from a tower system unit case*

Figure 2-7 *Removing the cover from a desktop system unit case*

In addition to the personnel safety precautions and the ESD hazard protection already discussed, several proper service practices should be followed while removing modules and components from the system unit case:

- Sketch and diagram all circuit board and cable placement, dip switch and jumper settings, and flat ribbon cable and connector orientation.

- Identify (ID) both ends of all cable connectors using matching ID tags.

- Avoid touching the edge connectors and components when removing circuit boards.

- Ensure that all circuit boards are completely seated before removing dust with a brush or compressed air.

The first step to cleaning circuit boards is not obvious: Reseat components in their sockets or circuit cards in their slots. This action is necessary to prevent poor electrical contact after completing the actual cleaning process, and variations to this step comprise three wrong answers on the A+ Core exam question regarding circuit board cleaning. Select the "the first cleaning step is to reseat components in their socket" answer.

Reassembling the System Unit Case

The following maintenance practices should be performed when reassembling the modules and components in the system unit case:

- Ensure that the # 1 pin or socket in the flat ribbon cable connector, which is indicated by the red edge of the flat ribbon cable, matches the # 1 pin or socket on the circuit board connector before mating the connectors. The pin or socket on the circuit board is identified by either a figure # 1 or a round solder connector next to the pin connector.

- Ensure that the red edge (# 1 conductor) on the flat ribbon cable is positioned toward the device's power connector, as depicted in Figure 2-8. This cable orientation ensures proper mating between the connectors.

- Ensure that all circuit boards are seated properly before replacing the system unit case cover.

- Ensure adequate cooling by reinstalling all parts on the case and keeping the case closed during operation to prevent overheating.

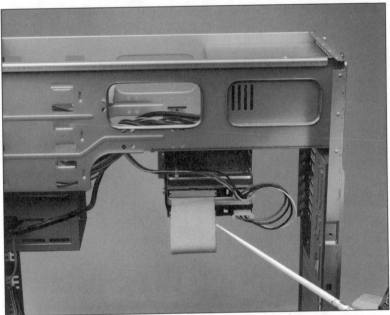

Figure 2-8 *A flat ribbon cable red edge (# 1 conductor) oriented toward the power connector*

Matching the #1 Pin and #1 Socket

For the A+ Core exam, you should know that the red edge conductor of a flat ribbon cable indicates the # 1 connector pin or socket, and it must match the opposite # 1 pin or socket of the connector on the system board or device before mating the connectors.

Recognize that all parts must be put back on the system unit case during re-assembly and that the case must remain closed during operation to prevent overheating.

Identifying Special Servicing Concerns

The environmental impact and fire hazards associated with performing computer servicing are major concerns. To address these concerns, special computer component disposal and fire fighting guidelines should be established.

Component Disposal

Several precautions must be followed when disposing of computer components and chemical substances. In most cases, you can use the manufacturer's Material Safety Data Sheet (MSDS) as a disposal guideline. Manufacturers are required by law to provide an MSDS, which identifies safety, hazard, and disposal information about each item manufactured or processed. Also consult the local EPA (Environmental Protection Agency) prior to disposing computer components and materials.

CRTs, batteries, and chemical cleaning solvents are examples of components and substances that require special disposal procedures according to either their MSDS or the local EPA requirements. Laser toner cartridges and toner kits, on the other hand, do not require special disposal procedures.

 There are several A+ Core exam questions on disposal measures. Familiarize yourself with the information an MSDS (Material Safety Data Sheet) covers. Also know which components require special disposal and which do not.

Fire Extinguishers

As with servicing any electromechanical device or system, fire prevention and protection must always be a primary concern when servicing computers. The BC-rated fire extinguisher that contains carbon dioxide is recommended for the computer-servicing environment. This is the fire extinguisher of choice for the following reasons:

- B-rated fire extinguishers are used for fires involving flammable liquids, such as grease and oil.
- C-rated fire extinguishers are used for fires involving *live* electrical equipment.
- Carbon dioxide, unlike dry chemical agents, does not damage equipment.

The A+ Core exam fire extinguisher question trap is the decision between using carbon dioxide or a dry chemical agent. Recognize that both are used in BC-rated fire extinguishers. However, carbon dioxide does not damage equipment and dry chemical agents do. The correct answer is clear: BC-rated fire extinguishers with carbon dioxide should be used in computer repair facilities.

Have You Mastered?

Now it's time to review the concepts in this chapter and apply your knowledge. These questions test your mastery of the material covered in this chapter.

1. Static electricity discharge occurs when objects:

☐ A. Are electrically ungrounded
☐ B. Have dissimilar electrical potentials
☐ C. Are electrically neutral
☐ D. Are electrically grounded

The correct answer is **B.** Static electricity is discharged when objects have dissimilar electrical potentials. Refer to the "Protecting Equipment from Electrostatic Discharge" section for more information.

2. What does the red edge conductor on flat ribbon cables indicate?

☐ A. The conductor is the negative wire.
☐ B. The conductor is the ground wire.
☐ C. The conductor is the power wire.
☐ D. The conductor is the # 1 wire.

The correct answer is **D.** The red edge conductor on flat ribbon cables identifies the # 1 wire. Refer to the "Reassembling the System Unit Case" section for more information.

3. What is used to clean the monitor's external plastic surfaces?

- ☐ A. A damp lint-free cloth and mild detergent
- ☐ B. Denatured alcohol
- ☐ C. Acetone
- ☐ D. A window cleaner

The correct answer is **A.** A slightly dampened lint-free cloth and mild detergent is recommended for cleaning the plastic surfaces of a computer module or device. Refer to the "Assembling a Basic Servicing Tool Kit" section for more information.

4. What does a parity error indicate?

- ☐ A. BIOS failure
- ☐ B. Operating system error
- ☐ C. Application system error
- ☐ D. RAM error

The correct answer is **A.** Most parity errors indicate a problem with the RAM. Refer to the "Identifying Error Codes and Problem Messages" section for more information.

5. Which of the following electronics in a CRT can retain a voltage even after the monitor has been shut off?

- ☐ A. Transistors
- ☐ B. Capacitors
- ☐ C. Anode circuitry
- ☐ D. Cathode circuitry

Both **B** and **C** are correct. Capacitors and the CRT anode circuitry can retain voltage even after power has been removed. Refer to the "Protecting Service Personnel from Electrical Shock and Laser Beams" section for more information.

6. CMOS chips can be damaged by voltages as low as:

- ☐ A. 15 volts
- ☐ B. 24 volts
- ☐ C. 10 volts
- ☐ D. 36 volts

The correct answer is **C.** CMOS integrated circuits are extremely sensitive to over-voltage and can easily be damaged from voltages as low as 10 volts. Refer to the "Protecting Equipment from Electrostatic Discharge" section for more information.

7. What is the first step in the modular servicing approach to servicing computers?

- ☐ A. Replace FRUs one at a time until the problem is corrected.
- ☐ B. Isolate the problem to a hardware or software module.
- ☐ C. Use a voltmeter to check system board and power supply voltages.
- ☐ D. Determine whether the power supply fan is work- ing. If not, replace the power supply.

The correct answer is **B.** The first step in the process is to isolate the problem to a hardware or software module. Refer to the "Defining Computer Module Servicing" section for more information.

8. CRTs can generate and retain a voltage as high as:

- ☐ A. 25,000 volts
- ☐ B. 10,000 volts
- ☐ C. 117 volts
- ☐ D. 48 volts

The correct answer is **A.** A CRT anode can build up voltages exceed- ing 25,000 volts. Refer to the "Protecting Service Personnel from Electrical Shock and Laser Beams" section for more information.

9. **Which of the following integrated circuit technology is the most susceptible to ESD damage?**

   ☐ A. TTL
   ☐ B. CMOS
   ☐ C. FET
   ☐ D. IGT

The correct answer is **B.** Chips made from CMOS technology are fast and require low power, but they are the most susceptible to ESD damage. Refer to the "Protecting Equipment from Electrostatic Discharge" section for more information.

10. **How do you check the functionality of an anti-static wrist strap?**

   ☐ A. Use a multimeter to check the voltage potentials
   ☐ B. Use a multimeter to check the current flow
   ☐ C. Use a multimeter to check the resistance
   ☐ D. Use a multimeter to check continuity

The correct answer is **C.** The resistance of an anti-static wrist strap should be 1 Megaohm at all times. Refer to the "Protecting Equipment from Electrostatic Discharge" section for more information.

System Unit Cases

THIS CHAPTER ADDRESSES system unit case styles and designs. It prepares you for A+ Core exam questions on serial and parallel ports as well as the other connectors commonly mounted on the back panel of the system unit case. After completing this chapter, you also will be able to answer questions on input/output (I/O) port Interrupt-Request (IRQ) settings and I/O addresses, and the Small Computer System Interface (SCSI) bus.

Exam Material in This Chapter

Based on the Official Objectives

- Identify common peripheral ports and associated cables and connectors
- Identify the unique features of portable computer systems
- Know how to configure IRQ settings and I/O addresses
- Identify proper procedures for installing and configuring SCSI devices

Based on the Author's Experience

- Understand the various features of the system unit case
- Expect several questions on serial and parallel ports
- Be able to identify the common connectors mounted on the case back panel
- Memorize the default IRQ settings and I/O addresses listed in Table 3-1
- Know about the unique features of portable computer components, such as PC Cards, docking stations, batteries, and liquid crystal diode (LCD) screens
- Anticipate questions about SCSI termination, cabling, and connectors
- Expect questions on the new universal serial bus (USB)
- Be able to identify common communication and network device connectors

Are You Prepared?

1. What is the default I/O setting for COM1?

- [ ] A. 02F8
- [ ] B. 03F8
- [ ] C. 02E8
- [ ] D. 0278

2. Which of the following is not a valid type of SCSI connector?

- [ ] A. 80-pin connector
- [ ] B. 36-pin Centronics
- [ ] C. 50-pin Centronics
- [ ] D. 68-pin connector

3. What type of connector is used to connect a modem to a telephone cable?

- [ ] A. BNC
- [ ] B. RJ-45
- [ ] C. RJ-11
- [ ] D. DB25

Answers:

1. B   *The default I/O address for COM1 is 03F8. See Table 3-1: "Default COM and LPT Port IRQ Settings and I/O Addresses."*

2. B   *A 36-pin Centronics connector is generally used on a parallel printer and never as a SCSI connector. The other connector types are commonly used as SCSI connectors. See the "Understanding the Small Computer System Interface Bus" section.*

3. C   *Modems use the standard telephone connector RJ-11. See the "Understanding I/O Ports and Identifying Back Panel Connectors" section.*

Recognizing System Unit Case Features

The design and construction of a system unit case can be likened to parts of the human body. The case, an external sheet metal cover, is the skin that protects the internal hardware devices from external environmental hazards. The case's internal chassis is the skeleton that provides hardware device support. The I/O port and other device connectors on the case's back panel are openings through which the computer communicates with the rest of the world.

The tower, desktop, and portable case are three system unit case styles. Each style incorporates designs and features that provide both advantages and disadvantages for the computer user.

Tower Cases

The tower is the most common system unit case style and has several advantages over the desktop and portable case designs. One advantage is its capability to contain many more mass storage devices, such as hard disk drives, CD-ROM drives, and removable disk drives. Tower cases also incorporate power supplies with higher power ratings. Another advantage to tower cases is that they provide better cooling, which improves electronic component reliability.

Tower case styles include the mini-tower, mid-tower, and full-tower. The configuration of the tower case is primarily determined by the form factor of the system board (also called the *motherboard* or the *main board*). For example, the newer ATX (Advanced Technology X) system board for the Pentium II microprocessor dictates that the case must also be an ATX-class configuration. Another common case configuration and system board form factor is called the Baby AT, which is two-thirds the size of the older Full AT case and system board.

Tower System Unit Cases

Advantages to tower system unit cases:

- Contain more devices
- Higher-rated power supplies
- Better cooling for improved component reliability
- Better maintainability

Disadvantages to tower system unit cases:

- Larger footprint
- Less stable

Desktop Cases

As with the tower case, the desktop case configuration is primarily determined by the form factor of the system board. Currently, the two most popular desktop case and system board configurations are the ATX and the Baby AT.

One advantage the desktop case has over the tower case is that it is more compact. The desktop system design has a smaller footprint, the surface area occupied by both the case and monitor, because the monitor is placed on top of the case rather than alongside it. Another advantage to the desktop case is that it is more stable and less likely to be knocked over.

Portable Computer Cases

Portable computer case styles, such as the laptop, notebook, and palm-top, have the obvious advantages in terms of portability and small footprint size. However, several major disadvantages to portable system designs include their relatively small active or passive liquid crystal display (LCD) screens and their need for frequent battery recharges. A portable computer's internal hardware devices are also difficult to upgrade because the case has limited space.

Portable computers often have active matrix LCD screens due to the inherent disadvantages of passive matrix LCD displays. Active matrix screens are brighter and the images are sharper than passive matrix screens, although they use more power. Passive matrix displays are less expensive, but typically they are limited in the resolution and the number of colors that can be displayed. Passive matrix screens also are much slower than active displays because the images are drawn on the screen line by line.

To reduce the battery recharging frequency, Advanced Power Management (APM) is usually employed in modern portable computer designs. APM automatically puts the portable into *sleep,* or *suspend,* mode after set periods of inactivity to conserve the battery charge.

Portable computers generally use either nickel metal hydride (NiMH) or nickel cadmium (NiCad) batteries. Although NiMH batteries have better charging characteristics, both battery types are interchangeable. In contrast, litium ion (Li-Ion) batteries should never be used as replacements for NiMH or NiCad batteries because Li-Ion batteries have different charging requirements and can explode if improperly charged.

Upgrading the portable computer from outside the case can be easily done using Personal Computer Memory Card International Association (PCMCIA) cards (also called *PC Cards*). PC Cards are credit-card size and can be inserted into a PC Card slot (also called a *PC Card drive* or a *PC Card reader*); this enables expansion hardware devices, such as additional memory modules, modems, Network Interface Cards (NICs), and mass storage devices to be employed.

PC Card slots are usually built into the side of the portable computer's case and work with implementing software (also called *software enablers*) or device drivers to communicate with the PC Cards. Software enablers automatically configure the hardware device settings. PC Cards can be replaced while the PC is still operating. This process is called *hot swapping.* PC Cards and slots are classified according to their size and functions:

- **Type I PC Cards** are 3.3 mm thick and provide additional memory.

- **Type II PC Cards** are 5 mm thick and support most hardware expansion devices, but they do not support portable hard disk drives.

- **Type III PC Cards** are 10.5 mm thick and support most hardware expansion devices, including portable disk storage drives.

Most new portable computers can accommodate all three PC Card types because Type III PC Card readers contain two slots stacked on top of each other in a single opening. This feature enables the user to insert either two Type I cards or two Type II cards, or only one Type III card.

Dongles are used on PC Card modems. They are cable extensions that attach PC Card modems to telephone line or local area network (LAN) connectors. Dongles are fragile and often cause communication problems between portable computers and networks or the Internet.

PC Card Characteristics

You should know that Type III PC Cards support most hardware expansion devices. Additionally, you should recognize that Type III PC Card readers can accommodate either two Type I or two Type II PC Cards, but only one Type III PC Card. Also know that PC Cards can be *hot swapped* or replaced without computer shutdown, and that *software enablers* must be loaded for PC Cards to function properly. Also be aware that faulty *dongles* cause portable computer communication problems.

A docking station is another unique component that can be used in a portable computer system. A docking station enables a portable computer to be plugged into a desktop computer to access its keyboard, disk drives, monitor, and printer.

Four A+ Core exam questions focus on the following portable computer topics: LCD screens, power management, batteries, PC Cards, docking stations, and dongles. Review these important subjects in this section so that you feel confident you can correctly answer the questions.

Understanding the System Unit Case Chassis

The system unit case chassis is the metal frame on which the printed circuit boards and other hardware devices are mounted. It also provides the framework to which the sheet metal covers and plastic front panel bezels are attached with fasteners. The back panel, which contains the I/O port and other device connectors, is often an integral part of the chassis, except for the new ATX-class system boards and cases. With the ATX-class case configuration, the connectors are mounted directly on the system board and extend through the case's back panel. Figure 3-1 is a typical tower system unit case chassis. Figure 3-2 is a typical desktop system unit case chassis.

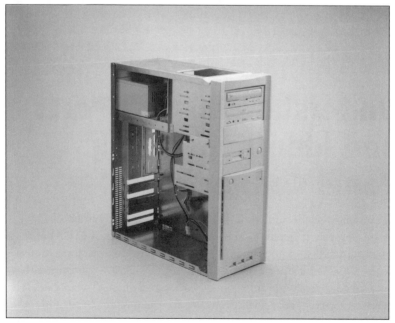

Figure 3-1 *Typical tower system unit case chassis*

Figure 3-2 *Typical desktop system unit case chassis*

Understanding I/O Ports and Identifying Back Panel Connectors

The standard connectors mounted on the back panel of an AT-class system unit case generally include a Video Graphics Array (VGA) or a Super VGA (SVGA) monitor connector, a keyboard connector, a mouse connector, a parallel port, and two serial ports. Figure 3-3 illustrates the standard connectors mounted on the back panel of an AT-class case. It is also common to have special connectors for the modem, SCSI, and LAN cables on the case's back panel.

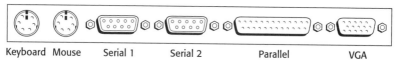

Keyboard Mouse   Serial 1   Serial 2   Parallel   VGA

Figure 3-3 *Standard connectors on the back panel of an AT-class case*

With the new Pentium II ATX-class case and system board configuration, the standard connectors are mounted directly on the system board rather than on the back panel. Two new USB ports are also mounted on the ATX-class system board. The USB standards' protocol permits 127 peripheral devices to be connected to one bus in a daisy-chain configuration. (A daisy chain is a set of hardware devices connected to each other in a serial arrangement.) Figure 3-4 depicts the ATX-class system board with the standard I/O port and other device connectors mounted directly on the board.

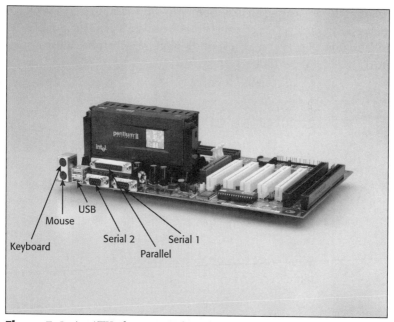

Figure 3-4 *An ATX-class system board with a mounted I/O port and other device connectors*

For the A+ Core exam, you should be able to identify common device and cabling connectors from either illustrations (such as Figure 3-3) or pictures (such as Figure 3-4).

Serial Ports and Connectors

Most computer operating systems (DOS-based) designate serial ports as COM (short for communications) plus a number to identify a specific serial port, such as COM1 and COM2. Serial ports are called COM ports because they provide a means for the hardware devices inside the system unit case to communicate with the serial hardware devices outside the case, such as mice, modems, and serial printers. The design standard that governs serial communications is RS-232, and serial ports are often referred to as RS-232 ports. Through serial ports, data is sent, received, and controlled either one bit at a time, or in serial fashion. Serial port connectors on the case's back panel are either male 9-pin D-subminiature (also called DB9) or male 25-pin D-subminiature (also called DB25).

 Characteristics of Serial Ports

For the A+ Core exam, know the following serial port characteristics:

- Serial (RS-232) ports communicate one bit of data at a time in both directions.
- Serial port connectors are either male DB9s or male DB25s.
- Serial ports support mice, modems, and serial printers.

Parallel Ports and Connectors

The operating system designates the parallel ports as LPT (for line printer). Parallel ports communicate simply and quickly, and they are commonly used to communicate with parallel printers. The design standard that governs parallel communications is IEEE-1284, and parallel ports are often called Standard Parallel Ports (SPPs). Parallel ports send eight bits or one byte of data simultaneously over eight separate wires in a single cable.

Parallel port connectors on the case's back panel are female 25-pin D-subminiature (DB25) connectors.

With a parallel printer cable, a DB25 connector is attached to one end and a 36-pin Centronix-type connector is attached to the other. A Centronix-type connector is usually mounted on most parallel printers.

Characteristics of Parallel Ports

For the A+ Core exam, know the following parallel port characteristics:

- Parallel (Centronix and IEEE-488) ports communicate eight bits or one byte of data at a time.

- Parallel port connectors are female DB25s.

- Parallel ports generally support parallel printers, which have a 36-pin Centronics connector to attach the printer cable between the printer and the LPT1 port's female DB25 connector.

COM and LPT Port IRQ Settings and I/O Addresses

All hardware devices communicate with the microprocessor through wires called IRQ lines that enable each device to receive attention from the microprocessor on a priority basis. Each device is also assigned an I/O address, enabling the microprocessor to determine where the device is located. Serial and parallel ports use only specific IRQ settings and I/O addresses, which are listed in Table 3-1.

Table 3-1 Default COM and LPT Port IRQ Settings and I/O Addresses

Port Type	IRQ Settings	I/O Addresses
COM1	IRQ4	03F8
COM2	IRQ3	02F8
COM3	IRQ4	03E8
COM4	IRQ4	02E8
LPT1	IRQ7	0378
LPT2	IRQ5	0278

Several A+ Core exam questions specifically ask about I/O port IRQ settings and I/O addresses. Memorize Table 3-1 and note that COM1 and COM3 both share IRQ4, and that COM2 and COM4 both share IRQ3.

Microsoft Diagnostics (MSD), a DOS utility program, can be used to view each I/O port and other hardware device IRQ settings and I/O addresses. In Windows 95, the Computer Properties Page on the Device Manager Property Sheet can be used to view hardware device IRQ settings and I/O addresses.

 True or False?

1. Li-Ion batteries can replace NiCad batteries.
2. Com ports communicate one bit of data and LPT ports communicate eight bytes of data at a time.
3. IRQ7 is the setting used with LPT1.

Answers: *1. False   2. False   3. True*

Monitor Connector

A three-row female DB15 connector (refer to Figure 3-3) is usually mounted on the slot plate of the VGA or SVGA video adapter card. Generally, it is the only connector on the plate.

Keyboard Connector

The 104-key PS/2-style, or *enhanced*, keyboards use miniature DIN-6 style connectors (refer to Figure 3-4). The 101-key IBM AT keyboards use DIN-5 connectors. They are slightly larger in diameter than the newer PS/2 style and contain one less pin.

Keyboards should never be removed or connected while the computer is operating because severe damage can occur to the supporting circuitry on the system board. Additionally, the keyboard and mouse connections must never be reversed during computer boot or operation.

Mouse Connector

Newer ATX-style and Baby AT-style system boards usually incorporate PS/2 mouse connectors to connect PS/2-type mice. A PS/2 mouse connector is the same as a PS/2 keyboard connector, and presents a potential problem if the mouse and keyboard connections are inadvertently reversed. Older computers used either a male DB9 serial port connector or a male DB25 connector on an I/O port expansion board to connect the mouse cable.

Keyboard and Mouse Improper Connections

Severe system board damage can occur if the keyboard is removed or if the mouse and keyboard connections are reversed during computer startup or operation.

Communication and Network Connectors

Several types of special connectors, such as the following, are used to connect telephone and network cables to modems and network adapter cards:

- **RJ-11** (Registered Jack-11) connectors are usually configured as pairs (labeled line and phone) and are used on internal and external modems to connect to telephone lines and telephone wall jacks.

- **RJ-45** (Registered Jack-45) connectors are used on network adapter cards to connect to 10base T Ethernet (twisted-pair) cabling in a LAN.

- **BNCs** (Bayonet Naur Connector, also called bayonet connector) are used on network adapter cards to connect coaxial cables in a LAN.

Understanding the Small Computer System Interface Bus

Small Computer System Interface (SCSI) connectors can also be mounted on the case's back panel to significantly expand the number of peripheral devices attached to the computer. Rather than attaching only a single hardware device to a serial or parallel port connector, multiple SCSI devices can be connected to a SCSI host adapter card connector mounted on the case's back panel.

Narrow (8-bit) SCSI-1 and Fast or Ultra (8-bit) SCSI-2 buses support up to eight SCSI devices, including the adapter card. Fast Wide or Wide Ultra (16-bit) SCSI-3 buses support up to 16 SCSI devices, including the adapter card.

SCSI buses support both internal and external hardware devices. The SCSI devices are attached together in a daisy chain or serial arrangement that is terminated at both ends by adding a resistor or other electrical scheme (enabled by a manual switch) on the chain's end devices.

When you answer A+ Core exam questions regarding the maximum number of SCSI devices that can be *supported* by a SCSI bus, don't forget to include the SCSI host adapter. However, when you answer a question regarding the maximum number of devices that can be *attached* to a SCSI bus, don't forget to exclude the SCSI host adapter. For example, a Fast Wide or Wide Ultra SCSI-3 bus can support up to 16 SCSI devices but only a maximum of 15 SCSI devices can be attached to the bus.

The SCSI devices are connected to a SCSI host adapter card, which is installed in either a Peripheral-Component Interconnect (PCI) or an Industry-Standard Architecture (ISA) expansion slot on the system board (see Figure 3-5). SCSI devices are attached together using either SCSI-1 or SCSI-2 50-conductor cables and 50-pin connectors, or SCSI-3 68-conductor cables and 68-pin connectors.

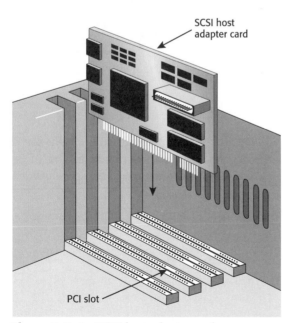

Figure 3-5 *An SCSI host adapter card*

Each device in the SCSI daisy chain must have its own individual address called an SCSI Identification (ID). The SCSI ID can be set from 0-7 for a narrow (8-bit) SCSI-1 and Fast or Ultra SCSI-2 buses, and 0-15 for a wide (16-bit) SCSI bus. SCSI IDs can be set either manually by using numeric selector switches on the SCSI device or automatically by the basic input/output system (BIOS) on the SCSI host adapter card. The SCSI ID for the host adapter card, which has the highest priority, is 7 for a narrow SCSI bus and 15 for a wide SCSI bus. Figure 3-6 depicts a typical SCSI device chain.

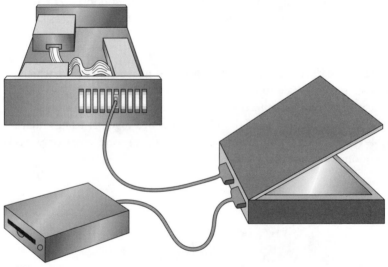

Figure 3-6 *A typical SCSI device chain*

The maximum physical lengths (or the total of all cable lengths connecting the external SCSI devices together) and maximum number of SCSI devices in single-ended SCSI buses cannot exceed the specifications shown in Table 3-2.

Table 3-2 SCSI Bus Specifications

SCSI Standard	Bus Width (Bits)	Transfer Rate (MB/Second)	Maximum Bus Length (Meters)	Maximum Device Support
Narrow SCSI-1	8	5	6	8
Fast SCSI-2	8	10	3	8
Ultra SCSI-2	8	20	1.5	8
Ultra SCSI-2	8	20	3	4
Fast Wide SCSI-3	16	20	3	16
Wide Ultra SCSI-3	16	40	1.5	8
Wide Ultra SCSI-3	16	40	3	4

TEST TIP

Be sure to memorize all the SCSI bus specifications in Table 3-2 for the A+ Core exam. Three or four questions specifically address these key SCSI specifications.

KNOW THIS

Installing and Configuring SCSI Devices

You should know the following key points about installing and configuring SCSI devices:

- SCSI cables, devices, and host adapter cards generally use 50-pin, 68-pin, and 80-pin connectors, respectively. (Apple/Mac and older Sun workstations use DB25 connectors.)

- Narrow SCSI-1 and Fast or Ultra (8-bit) SCSI-2 buses support up to eight SCSI devices, including the host adapter card.

Continued

- Fast Wide or Wide Ultra (16-bit) SCSI-3 buses support up to 16 SCSI devices, including the host adapter card.

- Double-ended SCSI chains must be terminated at both ends.

- Only one IRQ is required for a SCSI bus.

Have You Mastered?

Now it's time to review the concepts in this chapter and apply your knowledge. These questions test your mastery of the material covered in this chapter.

1. What is a primary and unique feature of PC Cards?

- ☐ A. They can be attached to both serial and parallel ports
- ☐ B. They can be *hot swapped*
- ☐ C. They can replace any other expansion or adapter card in a computer
- ☐ D. They optimize battery life

The correct answer is **B.** PC Cards can be changed out (also called *hot swapping*) while a portable computer is operating. Refer to the "Portable Computer Cases" section for more information.

2. What are the respective IRQ default settings for COM1 and COM2?

- ☐ A. IRQ1 and IRQ2
- ☐ B. IRQ3 and IRQ4
- ☐ C. IRQ4 and IRQ3
- ☐ D. IRQ2 and IRQ1

The correct answer **C.** IRQ4 is the default setting for COM1, and IRQ3 is the default setting for IRQ3. See Table 3-1: "Default COM and LPT port IRQ settings and I/O addresses" for more information.

3. Which statement is true regarding SCSI termination?

- [ ] A. Only disk drives must be terminated.
- [ ] B. Only the SCSI host adapter must be terminated.
- [ ] C. Both ends of the SCSI chain must be terminated.
- [ ] D. Termination is not necessary.

The correct answer is **C.** Devices at each end of a SCSI chain must be terminated. For more information, refer to the "Understanding the Small Computer System Interface Bus" section.

4. What are the respective default I/O addresses for LPT1 and LPT2?

- [ ] A. 03F8 and 02F8
- [ ] B. 0378 and 0278
- [ ] C. 7 and 5
- [ ] D. 03E8 and 03E8

The correct answer is **B.** 0378 is the default I/O address for LPT1 and 0278 is the default I/O address for LPT2. Refer to Table 3-1, "Default COM and LPT Port IRQ Settings and I/O Addresses," for more information.

5. Transferring a byte of data over eight individual wires simultaneously is called:

- [ ] A. Serial communications
- [ ] B. Parallel communications
- [ ] C. Network communications
- [ ] D. SCSI communications

The correct answer is **B.** Parallel ports communicate eight bits or one byte of data simultaneously. Refer to the "Parallel Ports and Connectors" section for more information.

6. **If a mouse is connected to COM2, which I/O port will accept an external modem?**

> ☐ A. LPT1
> ☐ B. LPT2
> ☐ C. COM1
> ☐ D. Serial3

The correct answer is **C.** A modem is a serial device and must be connected to a COM port. Refer to the "Serial Ports and Connectors" section for more information.

7. **LPT1 uses which connector?**

> ☐ A. Male DB9
> ☐ B. Male DB25
> ☐ C. Female DB15
> ☐ D. Female DB25

The correct answer is **D.** LPT1 port connectors use a female DB25 connector. Refer to the "Parallel Ports and Connectors" section for more information.

8. **Which connectors are used on Network Interface Cards for connecting to 10baseT Ethernet cabling (twisted-pair) and coaxial cables, respectively?**

> ☐ A. RJ-45 and BNC
> ☐ B. RJ-11 and BNC
> ☐ C. BNC and RJ-52
> ☐ D. RJ-52 and RJ11

The correct answer is **A.** RJ-45 and BNC connectors are used on network adapter cards to connect to 10baseT Ethernet cabling and coaxial cables, respectively. Refer to the "Communication and Network Connectors" section for more information.

9. **Which PC Card supports most hardware expansion devices, but not portable hard disk drives?**

     ☐ A. Type I
     ☐ B. Type II
     ☐ C. Type III
     ☐ D. Type IV

The correct answer is **B.** Type II PC Cards support most hardware expansion devices, with the exception of portable hard disk drives. Refer to the "Portable Computer Cases" section for more information.

10. **What is the maximum number of SCSI hardware devices that the Fast Wide SCSI-3 buses support, including the host adapter card?**

     ☐ A. 8
     ☐ B. 16
     ☐ C. 24
     ☐ D. 6

The correct answer is **B.** Wide or Fast Wide SCSI-3 buses support up to 16 devices. Refer to the "Understanding the Small Computer System Interface Bus" section for more information.

System Boards

THIS CHAPTER DISCUSSES the system board (also called the *motherboard*), which is the foundation of the computer. It presents vital information that you should know to answer A+ Core exam questions regarding system board styles, design, construction, and servicing requirements. After reviewing this chapter, you also will be able to correctly identify the primary electrical and mechanical components common in today's most popular system boards.

Exam Material in This Chapter

Based on the Official Objectives

- Identify the concepts and functions of system boards
- Identify the most popular types of system boards and their components
- Know how to service system boards

Based on the Author's Experience

- Understand the contrasting configurations and primary features of the ATX (Advanced Technology X) and Baby AT system boards
- Be able to identify all the components mounted on ATX and Baby AT system boards
- Anticipate questions regarding system board component functions
- Understand system or expansion bus architectures
- Anticipate questions regarding the functions, locations, and contents of the read-only memory (ROM) basic input/output system (BIOS) and Complementary Metal-Oxide Semiconductor (CMOS)
- Learn how to service and replace system boards
- Know how to change the hardware device settings in the CMOS using the System (also called BIOS or CMOS) Setup program in the ROM BIOS

Are You Prepared?

Test your knowledge with the following questions. Then you'll know if you're prepared for the material in this chapter or if you should review problem areas.

1. Which system board supports the Pentium II processors?

- ☐ A. Full AT
- ☐ B. Baby AT
- ☐ C. ATX
- ☐ D. IBM XT

2. After replacing a system board, what is the next step?

- ☐ A. Format the hard disk drive
- ☐ B. Run the MCD utility program
- ☐ C. Edit CONFIG.SYS
- ☐ D. Run the System Setup program

3. Classic Pentium processors are installed in what CPU connector mounted on the system board?

- ☐ A. Slot 7
- ☐ B. Socket 7
- ☐ C. Socket 4
- ☐ D. Slot 1

Answers:

1. C   *ATX system boards are specifically designed to support the Pentium II processors. See the "ATX system boards" section.*

2. D   *Following system board replacement, the System Setup program should be run to review and alter the hardware device configuration settings in the CMOS. See the "Servicing System Boards" section.*

3. B   *Classics Pentiums are installed in zero-insertion force (ZIF) Socket 7 connectors. See the "Baby AT system boards" section.*

Understanding System Boards

The system board or motherboard (also called the *main board* or *planar board*) is the most important printed circuit board (PCB) in the computer system. Acting as the foundation of the computer system, the system board is embedded and covered with a myriad of circuits, components, connectors, sockets, and slots. The system board also is the heart of the computer, bringing together all the other PCBs and components in the computer system. By installing expansion boards and adapter cards in the expansion slots on the system board, you can significantly enhance and expand a computer's capabilities.

System Board Design and Construction

The design and construction of the system board is similar to the other circuit boards in the computer system. The system board contains numerous integrated circuits (also called *chips*), resistors, capacitors, diodes, connectors, sockets, and slots mounted on a multi-layered core of nonconductive epoxy and fiberglass composite. The discrete components and parts are electrically connected by tiny copper foil traces (or imprints), forming hundreds of circuits that perform specific electronic and logic functions.

The core devices of the computer, which include the central processing unit (CPU) and random-access memory (RAM), are mounted on the system board using sockets and slots for easy replacement and upgrade. The components supporting the computer's core devices, such as the Flash BIOS, Level 2 Cache memory, the real-time clock (RTC) chip (which contains the CMOS), and the system board chip set, are usually soldered to the system board. System boards also contain several buses, which act as data highways that transport electronic signals among the components. Cables, flat ribbon cables, individual wires, and expansion slots and boards electrically connect the system board to the other circuit boards and devices inside and outside the system unit case.

System Board Form Factors

Form factors describe the size, shape, design, and component layout of electrical and mechanical devices. System boards are classified according to their form factors and include the ATX, Baby AT, and Full AT. Each of the system board types offers numerous contrasting designs and features ranging from the number and types of expansion slots to the types of CPU sockets or slots. The ATX is the most popular system board used by manufacturers of computers today. Figure 4-1 shows the contrasting size, shape, and design of the ATX, Baby AT, and Full AT system boards.

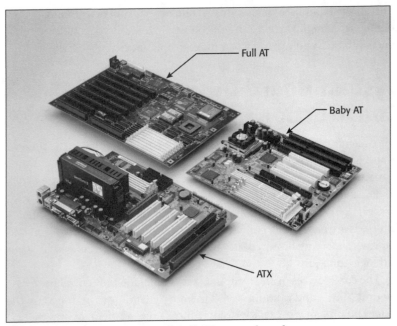

Figure 4-1 *ATX, Baby AT, and Full AT system boards*

Three or four A+ Core exam questions ask you to identify ATX and Baby AT system board form factors. Be able to recognize and compare the size, shape, design, and component layout of these two system board types. There are no questions on the exam that ask you to identify the Full AT form factors.

ATX system boards

Introduced by Intel in 1995, the ATX system board was designed to support the Pentium II processor. The ATX system board is 7.5-inches wide by 12-inches long. ATX system boards incorporate several improvements and advanced features that the older Baby AT and Full AT system boards do not have. Typical improvements and advanced features are integrated (on-board) I/O port and PS/2 mouse connectors, superior CPU cooling characteristics, Accelerated Graphics Port (AGP) local bus slot, and one or two universal serial bus (USB) ports. A 100MHz (megahertz) processor bus is an additional ATX feature that supports the 350 to 450MHz Pentium II (Deschutes), the 450 and 500MHz Pentium III CPUs, and many future Intel microprocessors. Most ATX system boards also incorporate a *soft power switch* feature that permits a selection of delay periods before the system is totally powered down.

Figure 4-2 shows the ATX system board with the Pentium II CPU installed in the CPU Slot 1 and the AGP video adapter card installed in the AGP local bus expansion slot. Figure 4-3 shows the ATX system board component layout.

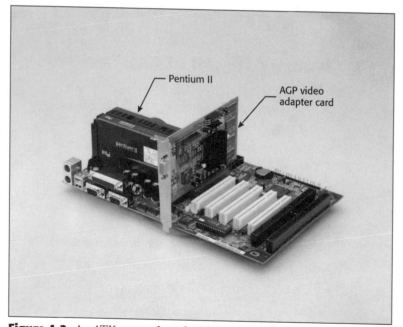

Figure 4-2 *An ATX system board with the Pentium II and AGP video adapter card installed in their respective connector slots*

Pentium classic
and cooling fan

Figure 4-3 *ATX system board component layout*

KNOW THIS Characteristics of ATX System Boards

The ATX system board incorporates the following improvements and advanced features:

- Slot 1 (supports the Pentium II, Pentium II, and Celeron CPUs)
- Integrated (on-board) I/O port and PS/2 mouse connectors
- AGP local bus
- Better cooling for improved component reliability
- *Soft power switch* (power-off timing feature)
- USB ports (each port can support up to 127 devices)

Baby AT system board

Until recently, the Baby AT was the most popular system board because of its small size and relatively advanced technological features that supported most of the latest hardware (except the Pentium II processor) for the time. The Baby AT is 8.5-inches wide by 10-inches long and two-thirds the size of a Full AT system board. Typical Baby AT system board features include the following:

- Zero-insertion force (ZIF) Socket 7 that supports 90-300MHz Pentium and Pentium-clone (AMD, Cyrix, and IDT) processors
- L2 cache memory
- Four single inline memory module (SIMM) slots
- Two dual inline memory module (DIMM) slots
- Intel Triton 430TX chip set
- Four 32-bit Peripheral-Component Interconnect (PCI) expansion slots
- Three 16-bit EISA (Enhanced Industry Standard Architecture) expansion slots
- Win95 and Win98 Plug-and-Play BIOS
- EIDE (Enhanced Integrated Drive Electronics) control
- Floppy drive control
- Direct memory access (DMA) controller
- PCI local bus, bus mastering, and EIDE bridging controllers
- PS/2 keyboard and mouse connectors

Figure 4-4 shows the Baby AT system board with the Classic Pentium processor and cooling fan installed in the ZIF Socket 7. Figure 4-5 shows the Baby AT system board component layout.

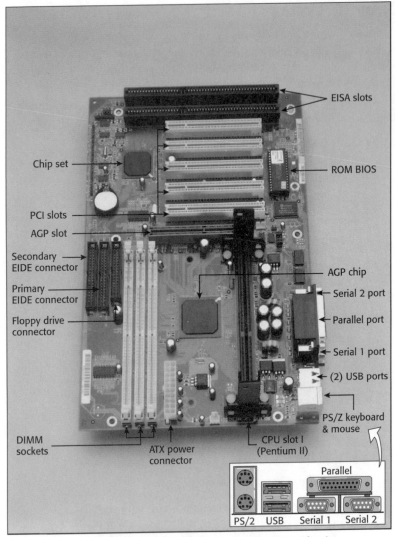

Figure 4-4 *A Baby AT system board with the Pentium Classic microprocessor and cooling fan installed in the ZIF Socket 7*

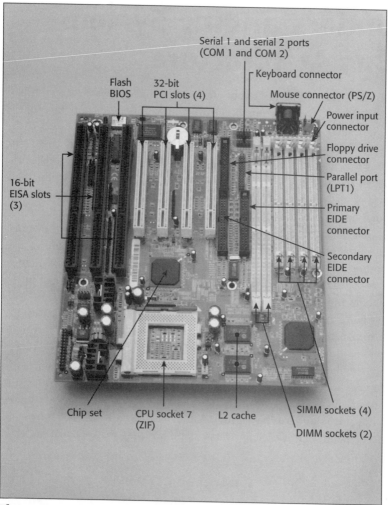

Figure 4-5 *A Baby AT system board component layout*

On the A+ Core exam, do not confuse the different ATX and Baby AT system board form factors when they are presented from different angles, such as three-quarter or plan (viewed from overhead). You should be able to identify the form factors regardless of the viewing angle. Refer to the previous five figures in this chapter for examples of various system board form factors.

Understanding System Bus Architectures

A bus is a common set of copper traces or signal highways on a circuit board that electrically connect the different components and parts of the system, such as the CPU, RAM, chip set, L2 cache memory, hard disk drive controllers, floppy drive controller, and expansion slots. The main buses on the system board include the processor bus, memory bus, and system (also called *input/output* or *expansion*) bus. Buses are further subdivided into specialized subgroups: data (word size) bus, address (locations) bus, and signal (control) bus.

Buses are generally categorized by the amount of data that they can transfer at one time, such as 8-bits, 16-bits, 32-bits, or 64-bits. Buses also are specified according to their clock signal rate in MHz, which synchronizes the data transfer rate or communication among the various components and devices on the bus.

Figure 4-6 is a typical system block diagram depicting the Pentium, system board chip set, system buses, RAM, and other CPU-supporting devices.

System or expansion buses connect the expansion boards and adapter cards in the expansion slots on the system board to the rest of the computer system (see the PCI bus in Figure 4-6). Various system bus architecture standards have evolved since the first IBM PC was introduced, including the seven primary standards that are discussed in the following sections.

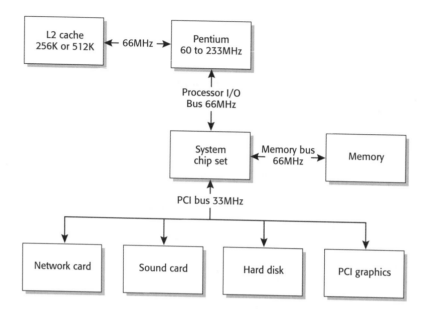

Figure 4-6 *A block diagram of the Pentium, system board chip set, system buses, RAM, and other CPU-supporting devices*

Industry Standard Architecture and Extended Industry Standard Architecture Buses

The 8-bit ISA was the original expansion bus standard used in the first IBM PC, introduced in 1981. When connectors were added to the Industry Standard Architecture (ISA) expansion slot design, the 8-bit ISA evolved into a 16/32-bit Extended Industry Standard Architecture (EISA) bus standard with the release of the Intel 80286 processor in 1984. EISA is backward compatible so that the 8-bit legacy ISA expansion cards can be installed in the 16-bit EISA expansion slots. Both ISA and EISA system buses have an 8MHz bus speed.

Peripheral Component Interconnect Local Buses

The 32/64-bit data path, 33MHz PCI local bus is the new design standard for most Pentium-type system board expansion slots and system bus architectures. The PCI expansion bus standard allows up to ten PCI expansion cards to be installed in a computer system. The PCI local bus is self-configuring for Plug-and-Play functionality, helping Windows 95 and Windows 98 detect and configure Plug-and-Play expansion cards when they are installed in PCI expansion slots. It also supports bus mastering, which enables *intelligent* PCI-compliant adapter cards to perform tasks independently of the CPU.

System boards often contain both EISA and PCI expansion slots, but during the next few years, system board manufacturers will stop incorporating EISA slots in their designs.

 Several A+ Core exam questions ask you to identify both EISA and PCI expansion slots. Review Figures 4 and 5 to understand the physical differences between the two types of expansion slots. Note that the EISA expansion slots are longer than the PCI slots.

Video Electronic Standards Association Local Buses

The 32-bit Video Electronic Standards Association (VESA) local bus was developed in 1992 to communicate with the CPU at the CPU's speed. The VESA standard allowed for up to three slots to be built into a system board, and it also facilitated bus mastering. The VL-bus, a version of the local bus, was developed specifically to accelerate video display signals. The outdated VESA local bus and VL-bus technology have been replaced by the new PCI local bus architecture.

Accelerated Graphics Port Local Bus

The 66MHz Accelerated Graphics Port (AGP) provides a direct path from the CPU to the graphics accelerator rather than through the 33MHz PCI local bus. The graphics accelerator relocation provides more full-featured and faster graphics performance. All ATX and some newer Baby AT system boards provide an AGP local bus slot.

The Universal Serial Bus

The universal serial bus (USB) is a new local bus that supports up to 127 peripheral devices at a data transfer rate of 12Mbps (Megabits per second). New computers usually incorporate either one or two USB phone-jack-size connectors on the system unit case's back panel. Peripherals such as a keyboard, monitor, or mouse can be plugged into a USB jack, and installation and configuration is completely automatic. Hubs can be added in the USB device chain to create a tiered-star arrangement of additional peripherals such as USB scanners and USB video cameras. Devices can also be removed or installed while the computer is operating, which is a feature called *hot-swapping*.

The Personal Computer Memory Card International Association

The 16-bit PC Card or Personal Computer Memory Card International Association (PCMCIA) bus architecture was developed by a group of portable computer manufacturers and vendors to promote a common standard for PC Card-based peripherals and the slots in the side of the case designed to hold them. For more information regarding the PCMCIA bus, see the "Portable Computer Cases" section in Chapter 3.

A+ Core exam questions focus on the following expansion bus topics: EISA bus speed (8MHz) and width (16/32-bits), PCI bus speed (33MHz) and width (32/64-bits), the number of devices supported by USB (127 devices), and PCMCIA bus characteristics (see Chapter 3). Note that the PCI local bus is much faster than the EISA bus, and that the USB design standard enables a huge number of peripheral devices to be attached to a computer system.

True or False?

1. EISA buses have a 16/32-bit width and 8MHz speed architecture.

2. ATX system boards incorporate Slot 7 for the Pentium II processor.

3. PCI local bus architecture is the new standard for today's expansion buses.

Answers: *1. True   2. False   3. True*

Understanding the ROM BIOS Chip

The read-only memory (ROM) basic input/output system (BIOS) chip is one of the most critical components on the system board. Together with the Complementary Metal-Oxide Semiconductor (CMOS), which is part of the real-time clock (RTC) chip, ROM BIOS plays a central role in testing, monitoring, and controlling the computer's hardware devices. It also initiates loading of the computer's operating system and acts as the *traffic cop* between the operating system (OS) and the hardware devices.

The ROM BIOS chip consists of both hardware and software, and it is often called *firmware*. ROM is long-term, non-volatile physical memory that stores the BIOS. The BIOS is the software instruction set that runs the power-on self test (POST), initiates loading of the operating system into RAM, runs the System (also called CMOS or BIOS) Setup program, and enables communication between the CPU and system hardware devices. It also contains the lowest-level system device drivers.

CMOS on the RTC chip works hand-in-hand with the ROM BIOS. It provides the basic hardware device information and configuration settings required by the ROM BIOS, CPU, and other hardware devices. During system setup (usually required following a hard disk drive or system board replacement), the System Setup program in the ROM BIOS provides a gateway for reviewing and altering the device settings in the CMOS. You can usually open the System Setup program during the boot sequence by following the on-screen instructions immediately following POST.

The RTC chip also contains the time and date memory registers (seconds, minutes, days, months, years, and millennium). The RTC chip, like main memory, is essentially dynamic random-access memory (DRAM), but DRAM, unlike main memory, requires very low power to maintain its stored data; main memory requires more power and constant power refreshment. Small, coin-size nickel cadmium batteries usually power newer RTC chips.

Many of the ROM BIOS chips currently manufactured are electrically erasable programmable read-only memory (EEPROM); this enables them to be erased and rewritten by software. The feature of upgrading the BIOS using software rather than replacing the ROM BIOS chip is called *Flash BIOS*. Flash BIOS can be upgraded using software on floppy diskettes or downloaded from the Internet.

Another new feature of ROM BIOS chips is Plug-and-Play (PnP) functionality. PnP is a hardware/software standard that enables the operating system to automatically recognize and configure PnP hardware devices. For a computer to be PnP functional, the hardware device, ROM BIOS, and operating system (such as Windows 95 and Windows 98) must be PnP.

Recognize that some video adapter cards, SCSI cards, and hard disk drive controllers also contain ROM BIOS chips. On the A+ Core exam, do not confuse the computer's main system ROM BIOS with a peripheral hardware device's ROM BIOS. The exam questions address only the system ROM BIOS.

ROM BIOS and CMOS

You should know that the ROM BIOS chip (also called firmware) contains the POST, Bootstrap Loader program, basic system device drivers, and System (also called BIOS or CMOS) Setup program. Newer ROM BIOS chips include Flash and Plug-and-Play features. Also know that the CMOS is located on the battery-powered RTC chip and contains hardware device information and configuration settings. Additionally, know that one beep during the boot sequence indicates that POST has not discovered any errors in the basic computer system.

Servicing System Boards

Several maintenance issues regarding system boards are important to learn for the A+ Core exam. They include diagnosing and isolating a typical system board problem, replacing a system board, and setting up the device configuration settings in the CMOS following a system board replacement. A typical system board problem-resolution scenario follows:

1. **Problem symptoms.** The computer does not boot (start up). It still does not boot after you install a bootable diskette in drive A and you attempt a reboot. Additionally, during the attempted start sequences, the fan in the power supply operates, and the power and hard disk drive indicator lights flash on.

2. **Problem isolation.** First, attempt to isolate the problem by checking the voltage output from the power supply (+/- 5 volts and +/- 12 volts). Then remove the expansion boards (except the video adapter card) one at a time, and reboot after you remove each board. If the computer fails to boot, sequentially replace the CPU, RAM, and ROM BIOS chip (unless it is a Flash ROM BIOS and the chip is soldered to the board), and attempt to reboot after each field replaceable unit (FRU) replacement.

3. **Problem resolution.** Because all the FRUs that can be easily replaced have been swapped out and the computer still fails to

boot, the system board should be replaced to resolve the problem.

4. **System board setup.** Setup of the system board prior to installation into the system unit case usually involves reinstalling the CPU and RAM on the new board and may require manually configuring the CPU power and speed jumper settings on the board. Some newer system boards provide a capability in the BIOS to configure the settings using software. The manual that accompanies the system board replacement kit provides step-by-step setup instructions for these tasks.

5. **New system board installation.** Once the system board is set up, it can be easily installed in the system unit case. Figure 4-7 shows a Full AT system board being installed into its Full AT system unit case. Figure 4-8 shows the ATX system board attached to the chassis side panel and positioned for installation into its ATX system unit case. Figure 4-9 is an ATX system board installed in its ATX system unit case.

Figure 4-7 *A Full AT system board being installed into its Full AT case*

Figure 4-8 *An ATX system board attached to the chassis side panel and positioned for installation into its ATX case*

Figure 4-9 *An ATX system board installed in its ATX case*

6. System setup. Finally, review and alter the peripheral hardware device settings in the CMOS using the System Setup program in the BIOS. You can open the System Setup program during the computer boot sequence by following the on-screen instructions. Current System Setup programs enable you to automatically or manually alter the following typical hardware device settings in the CMOS:

- Date
- Time
- Hard disk drives
    - Type
    - Size
    - Number of cylinders
    - Number of heads
    - Landing zones
    - Number of sectors
    - Modes (configuration) — including, Auto, Normal, Large, and Logical block addressing (LBA)
- Floppy disk drive type A/B
    - 3.5-inch
    - 5.25-inch
- Video
- Memory
- BIOS feature setup
- Chipset feature setup
- Power management setup
- PCI configuration setup
- EIDE configuration setup
- Security (password settings)

For the A+ Core exam, do not confuse the functions of CMOS and BIOS. CMOS contains only device configuration settings. The CMOS, or System Setup program, is actually in the BIOS and can be opened only during the boot sequence. Additionally, several questions ask specifically about the device setting changes that can be made in the CMOS using the System Setup program. Memorize the device settings from the above list.

Have You Mastered?

Now it's time to review the concepts in this chapter and apply your knowledge. These questions test your mastery of the material covered in this chapter.

1. A PCI expansion bus slot transfers how many data bits at one time?

- ☐ A. 8
- ☐ B. 16
- ☐ C. 32
- ☐ D. 128

The correct answer is **C.** A PCI bus slot transfers 32-bits of data at one time, whereas an EISA bus slot transfers 16-bits and an ISA bus slot transfers 8-bits. Refer to the "Understanding System Bus Architectures" section for more information.

2. What system board incorporates a *soft power switch* feature?

- ☐ A. Baby AT
- ☐ B. ATX
- ☐ C. Full AT
- ☐ D. PBX

The correct answer is **B.** ATX system boards incorporate a *soft power switch* feature that places the system in a sleep-mode before it is completely powered down. Refer to the "Understanding System Boards" section for more information.

3. How many peripheral devices can a USB support?

☐ A. 8
☐ B. 64
☐ C. 16
☐ D. 127

The correct answer is **D.** A single USB can support 127 devices in any sequence at 12Mbps. See the "Understanding System Bus Architectures" section for more information.

4. ROM BIOS is also called?

☐ A. Software
☐ B. Firmware
☐ C. Rite-ware
☐ D. Program-ware

The correct answer is **B.** ROM BIOS is often called firmware because it is considered half way between hardware and software in physical and non-physical form. Refer to the "Understanding the ROM BIOS Chip" section for more information.

5. Which system board contains an AGP?

☐ A. ATX
☐ B. Full AT
☐ C. Baby AT
☐ D. LPX

The correct answer is **A.** ATX system boards incorporate the AGP, which provides video adapter cards direct access to the CPU for faster graphics performance. Refer to the "Understanding System Boards" section for more information.

6. Which of the following is the most popular system board today?

☐ A. Baby AT
☐ B. Full AT
☐ C. ISA
☐ D. ATX

The correct answer is **D.** ATX is the most popular system board among computer manufacturers today. Refer to the "Understanding System Boards" section for more information.

7. Which of the following is the fastest system bus?

☐ A. ISA
☐ B. EISA
☐ C. PCI
☐ D. VL-bus

The correct answer is **C.** PCI is the fastest system bus with a 32/64-bit data path and bus speed of 33MHz. Refer to the "Understanding System Bus Architectures" section for more information.

8. The CMOS is located on which chip?

☐ A. RTC
☐ B. ROM
☐ C. BIOS
☐ D. RAM

The correct answer is **A.** CMOS is usually a 64K section of the battery-powered RTC chip. Refer to the "Understanding the ROM BIOS Chip" section for more information.

9. The CMOS contains which of the following?

☐ A. POST
☐ B. Hardware device settings
☐ C. Bootstrap Loader program
☐ D. System Setup program

The correct answer is **B.** CMOS contains the system's hardware device settings, which are accessed through the System Setup program in the ROM BIOS. Refer to the "Understanding the ROM BIOS Chip" section for more information.

10. The BIOS contains which of the following? (Choose all that apply.)

☐ A. POST
☐ B. Bootstrap Loader program
☐ C. Hardware device settings
☐ D. ROM

Both **A** and **B** are correct. The BIOS contains the POST and Bootstrap Loader program, whereas the ROM is the physical form of the chip itself and the CMOS contains the hardware device settings. Refer to the "Understanding the ROM BIOS Chip" section for more information.

Central Processing Units

T HIS CHAPTER EXAMINES the central processing unit (CPU), which is often called the brain of the computer. It prepares you for A+ Core exam questions concerning CPU design, packaging, performance, and classification. This chapter also presents you with important A+ Core exam information regarding the various features and performance characteristics of the Intel family of processors and their associated CPU sockets or slots on the system board.

Exam Material in This Chapter

Based on the Official Objectives

- Identify basic terms, concepts, and functions of CPUs
- Identify basic characteristics of popular CPUs
- Know how to service CPUs

Based on the Author's Experience

- Be able to identify the major CPU manufacturers and facts about the microprocessor industry and marketplace
- Expect questions on CPU design and packaging principles
- Memorize all the CPU specifications and features presented in Table 5-1
- Learn the definitions of the following terms: CPU speed, system bus speed, data bus width, and address bus width
- Be able to identify the most popular CPU sockets and slots
- Know the basic procedures and precautions to follow when replacing CPUs

Are You Prepared?

Test your knowledge with the following questions. Then you'll know if you're prepared for the material in this chapter or if you should review problem areas.

1. **Which CPU socket or slot on the system board is used to retain and support Pentium II processors?**

   ☐ A. Slot 7
   ☐ B. Slot 1
   ☐ C. Socket 7
   ☐ D. Socket 1

2. **What is the L2 cache memory capacity typically available for use by the Pentium II processor?**

   ☐ A. 64K
   ☐ B. 256K
   ☐ C. 512K
   ☐ D. 1MB

3. **What is the system board CPU socket or slot that contains 321 pin-sockets in a square pin-socket array that supports processors with power requirements of 2.5 to 3.3 volts?**

   ☐ A. Slot 1
   ☐ B. Socket 7
   ☐ C. Socket 8
   ☐ D. Socket 3

Answers:

1. B   *CPU Slot 1 and the Pentium II retention yoke assembly are used to electrically connect and mechanically retain the Pentium II processor to the system board. See the "Identifying CPU Sockets and Slots" section.*

2. C   *512K of L2 cache memory is available to the Pentium II processor. See Table 5-1, "Summary of Intel CPU Specifications and Features."*

3. B   *Socket 7 is the CPU socket that contains 321 pin-sockets in a square pin-socket array and that supports processors with power requirements of 2.5 to 3.3 volts. See the "Identifying CPU Sockets and Slots" section.*

Understanding CPUs

If you think of the system board or motherboard as the computer's heart, then the CPU is its brain. This vital integrated circuit (IC), or chip, interprets and executes program instructions and transfers data and information among the other system devices and resources. Together, the RAM and CPU constitute the core devices of the computer. All other computer system devices are peripheral. The computer's central core power dictates not only computer performance, but also, often, computer cost. Additionally, the CPU and RAM determine how system hardware devices are configured and which operating system and application programs are used.

CPUs contain ultra-large-scale integration (ULSI) circuits with millions of transistors that are fabricated on a single chip of either silicon crystal or another semiconductor material. They are housed in either a square ceramic pin grid array (PGA) package or a rectangular plastic single-edge-contact (SEC) cartridge. The Intel 386, 486, Classic Pentium, Pentium Pro, and Pentium MMX processors use the PGA package, and the Pentium II and Pentium III processors are housed in the SEC cartridge. A Celeron CPU uses a modified SEC cartridge. Figure 5-1 shows the Intel Pentium II SEC cartridge and the Classic Pentium, 486, and 386 processor PGA packages.

Figure 5-1 *An Intel Pentium II SEC cartridge and Classic Pentium, 486, and 386 processor PGA packages*

CPU Packaging

Intel CPUs are housed in either the single-edge-contact (SEC) cartridge or the pin grid array (PGA) package. Pentium II and Pentium III processors are housed in the SEC cartridge, whereas many of the pre-Pentium II processors use the PGA package.

The Microprocessor Marketplace

Intel is clearly the leader in designing and manufacturing CPUs with approximately 85 percent of the world's microprocessor market. Notable Intel CPU-compatible (clone) competition include Advanced Micro Devices (AMD), Cyrix (National Semiconductor), and IDT microprocessors. Motorola also is a major manufacturer of processors for Apple's product line of computers.

Intel processors have evolved through six generations since the introduction of the 8080 in 1974. The Pentium III 450MHz and 500MHz are the latest processors in the current generation of Intel processors. Table 5-1 summarizes the specifications and features of the primary Intel processors.

Table 5-1 Summary of Intel CPU Specifications and Features

Processor	Year Introduced	Clock Speed (MHz)[1]	System Bus Speed (MHz)[2]	Data Bus Width (Bits)[3]	Address Bus Width (Bits)[4]	External Power Requirements (Volts)	L1 Cache (On-board CPU)[5]	L2 Cache (Usually external to CPU)[6]
80386[7]	1985	16–33	CPU speed	16, 32	32	5	None	None
80486[7]	1989	25–100	25, 33, 50	32	32	5, 3.3[8]	8K, 16K	128K, 256K
Classic Pentium P5 (586)	1993	60–200	50, 60, 66	64	32	5, 3.3[9]	16K	256K, 512K
Pentium Pro P6 (686)	1995	150–200	60, 66	64	36	3.3	16K	256K, 512K, 1MB
Pentium MMX	1997	166–266	66	64	32	3.3	32K	256K, 512K
Pentium II (66MHz bus)	1998	233–333	66	64	36	2.8	32K	512K
Pentium II (100MHz bus)	1998	350–450	100	64	36	2.0	32K	512K
Celeron	1998	266–466	66	64	36	2.8	32K	128K

Continued

Table 5-1 *continued*

Processor	Year Introduced	Clock Speed (MHz)[1]	System Bus Speed (MHz)[2]	Data Bus Width (Bits)[3]	Address Bus Width (Bits)[4]	External Power Requirements (Volts)	L1 Cache (On-board CPU)[5]	L2 Cache (Usually external to CPU)[6]
Pentium III	1999	450–500	100	64	36	2.0	32K	512K
Merced	2000	800–1200 (est.)	100	64	64	2.0	64K (est.)	1MB (est.)

[1] *CPU Speed and* [2] *System Bus Speed: CPU performance is often equated to its clock speed (internal speed), which is a multiple of the timing pulse rate generated by the system clock circuit on the system board. A CPU is further defined by its external speed, which is the pulse rate of the system bus. For example, the clock multiplier circuit triples the system clock circuit pulse rate of 66MHz, providing a timing pulse rate of 200MHz to the Classic Pentium while its system bus timing frequency remains at 66MHz. (Additionally, the system pulse rate is halved to 33MHz, providing a timing frequency to the PCI bus.)*

[3] *Data Bus Width and* [4] *Address Bus Width: Data bus width (or size) is the maximum number of data bits that can moved into or out of the processor in one cycle or operation. Address bus width (or size) is the maximum amount of RAM that a processor can address.*

[5] *L1 Cache and* [6] *L2 Cache Memory: Cache is a special memory subsystem in which frequently used data values are duplicated for quick access. L1 Cache memory is internal to the CPU (on-board), and L2 Cache memory is usually external to the CPU and slower than L1 Cache. However, the Pentium Pro and Celeron processors are exceptions. Their L2 Cache memory is internal to the processor.*

[7] *Math Coprocessor: The Intel 486DX and newer processors have on-board floating-point processor capability, which enables floating-point arithmetic to significantly speed up processing and graphics. The 486SX and older processors use a separate math coprocessor, usually designated with one number higher than the processor. For example, the math coprocessor for the 80386DX processor is designated as the 80387.*

[8] *486DX4 external voltage requirement is 3.3 volts, not 5 volts like the other 486 processors.*

[9] *Classic Pentiums, 60 and 66MHz, require 5 volts of power, whereas all other Classic Pentiums need a 3.3 volt power supply.*

Four or five A+ Core exam questions regarding CPUs focus on the contrasting specifications and features among Intel processors. To prepare for these questions, memorize the CPU specifications and features in Table 5-1. Specifically, notice that the 80486DX (see note 7) offered the first integrated math coprocessor and that the 80486 provided the first L1 on-board cache memory. Additionally, observe that the Pentium Pro has a 64-bit data bus and 256K, 512K, and 1MB of L2 on-board cache memory.

To address the rapidly growing multimedia marketplace, in 1997, Intel introduced the Pentium MMX (MultiMedia Extensions), which contains 57 instructions that enhance voice, video, and graphics capabilities. MMX also provides single-instruction, multiple-data (SIMD) technology. SIMD enables one instruction to control multiple operations. Subsequent releases of Pentium CPUs also contain MMX technology.

Several A+ Core exam answer choices reference non-Intel processors, such as AMD's K6 and K7 and Cyrix's 6X86. Recognize that these choices are probably wrong answers and are probably used in an attempt to confuse you. The exam focus is on Intel CPUs.

Understanding Features of the Pentium II

The Pentium II (Deschutes) CPU, with a 100MHz processor bus speed, represents the latest family of Intel processors and incorporates several important advanced features that the older CPU families do not. Supported by the Intel 440 BX system-logic chip set, the Pentium II (Deschutes) CPU processor bus speed is increased from 66MHz to 100MHz, providing 60 percent more bandwidth to the system RAM. The L2 cache memory bandwidth also is increased from 66MHz to half the speed of the processor. Together with the new SDRAM, the increased bandwidth of the main buses significantly improves the overall performance of the processor over both the Pentium II with a 66MHz processor bus speed and older CPUs. Figure 5-2 presents a system block diagram of the CPU, system board chip set, system buses, SDRAM, and other Pentium II CPU-supporting devices.

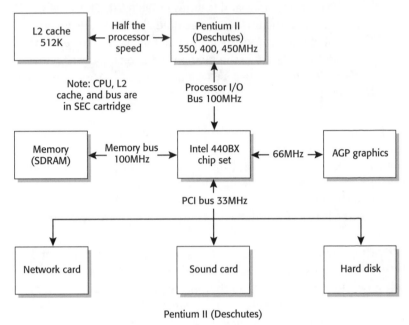

Pentium II (Deschutes)

Figure 5-2 *The system board chip set, system buses, SDRAM, and other devices supporting the Pentium II (Deschutes) CPU*

Other Pentium II (Deschutes) improvements include lowering the power supply voltage to 2 volts from 2.8 volts and reducing the physical circuit size inside the CPU from 0.35-micron to 0.25-micron. Future Intel processors, such as the Merced, will reduce the physical circuit size to 0.18-micron.

Features of the Pentium II (Deschutes)

You should know the following Pentium II (Deschutes) processor features:

- Increased clock speed: 350-450MHz
- Increased processor bus speed: 100MHz
- Increased L2 cache speed: 50 percent of processor speed
- Reduced circuit size: 0.25-micron
- Reduced power supply requirement: 2.0 volts

Identifying CPU Sockets and Slots

Intel and Intel-clone processors are electrically connected and mechanically retained to the system board with either socket or slot connectors on the system board. CPU socket connectors are usually square, whereas CPU slot connectors are narrow and long. Current socket and slot connector designs also include features that both enable easy CPU replacement and ensure positive electrical connection and mechanical retention.

CPU Sockets

CPU socket connectors contain hundreds of pin-sockets that are usually configured in a symmetrical, square pattern. Processors that are housed in PGA packages, such as the Classic Pentiums and 80486 processors, use sockets. Intel-clone CPUs also use sockets. Figure 5-3 illustrates a typical CPU socket design. Note that there are numerous female pin-sockets to complement the male CPU pins.

Figure 5-3 *A typical CPU socket design*

Newer CPU sockets incorporate a zero-insertion force (ZIF) design to ease the task of inserting or removing the processors. A built-in handle also eliminates the need for special tools and reduces the possibility of damage during CPU replacement. You simply lift the handle, place the processor into the socket, and then close the handle. Figure 5-4 illustrates a ZIF CPU socket design. Note that the handle is in the raised and unlocked position.

Figure 5-4 *A ZIF CPU socket design*

The most common CPU sockets currently used on system boards are as follows:

- **CPU Socket 3:** The Intel CPU socket supports the Intel 80486 processors. It contains 237 pin-sockets and supplies 5 volts to power most models of the 486 processor. It also provides 3.3 volts (by changing jumper settings on the system board) to power the 486DX4 processors.

- **CPU Socket 5:** Providing 3.3 volts power supply, the Socket 5 contains 320 pin-sockets to support 75 to 133MHz Classic Pentium processors. It is an upgrade from Socket 4, which supplies 5 volts to power only 60 and 66MHz Classic Pentiums. CPU Socket 5 has been replaced by Socket 7.

- **CPU Socket 6:** The 235 pin-socket CPU Socket 6 was also designed to support 486 processors and intended as an upgrade to Socket 3. However, because 486 processors were phased out of the marketplace, Socket 6 never went into production.

- **CPU Socket 7:** CPU Socket 7 is currently the industry standard and the most popular CPU socket for processors other than Pentium II, Pentium III, and Celeron CPUs. It supports Classic Pentiums from 7 to 200MHz, Pentiums with MMX Technology, and most sixth-generation processors manufactured by AMD, Cyrix, and IDT.

  Socket 7 contains 321 pin-sockets and supplies a regulated power supply (using the voltage regulator module, or VRM) of 2.5 to 3.3 volts, which can be selected by manually changing jumpers on the system board or using software in the BIOS.

- **CPU Socket 8:** The Pentium Pro processor uses the CPU Socket 8. Socket 8 contains 387 pin-sockets and supplies 3.1 and 3.3 volts to the processor. It is extremely large in order to accommodate the SPGA packaging design used by the Pentium Pro. The extra pins are used by the chip set to control the L2 cache memory that is integrated in the SPGA package rather than mounted on the system board.

CPU Slot 1

The CPU Slot 1, which is used for Pentium II, Pentium III, and Celeron processors, has a totally different connector design compared to the square PGA design of the socket series of CPU connectors. The Pentium processor's relatively thin, rectangular SEC cartridge design contains a small circuit board on which the P6 processor and 512K of L2 cache are mounted; this provides a faster data transfer than if the L2 cache were mounted outside the cartridge on the system board.

CPU Slot 1 has 242 pin-sockets to receive the SEC cartridge edge-connector pins. It also supplies 2.0 volts of regulated power supply to the Pentium II and Pentium III 100MHz bus processors, and it supplies 2.8

volts to the Celeron and Pentium II 66MHz bus processors. A plastic retention-yoke assembly mechanically attaches the Pentium II to Slot 1 and the system board. Figure 5-5 depicts the Pentium II mounted in the CPU Slot 1 on the system board.

Figure 5-5 *A Pentium II installed in CPU Slot 1*

CPU Sockets and Slots

You should know the following key points regarding CPU sockets and slots:

- Pentium II processors use the 242 pin-socket CPU Slot 1.

- Pentium MMX, Classic Pentium (from 75 to 200MHz), and sixth-generation Pentium-clone processors use the 321 pin-socket CPU Socket 7.

- Pentium Pro processors use the 387 pin-socket CPU Socket 8.

- Intel 80486 processors use the 237 pin-socket CPU Socket 3.

- Intel 80486DX4 processors require 3.3 rather than 5 volts power.

Additionally, you should know the power supply requirements for all the Intel processors. See Table 5-1, "Summary of Intel CPU Specifications and Features" for reference.

Installing CPUs

You should follow several proper procedures and should exercise caution when installing CPUs into their associated slots or sockets. For example, you must first install the Pentium II retention yoke assembly into Slot 1 on the system board (see Figure 5-6) before installing the Pentium II processor (see Figure 5-7) into the retention yoke assembly.

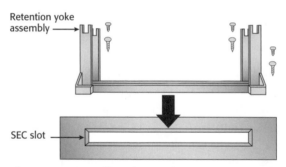

Figure 5-6 *Installing the Pentium II retention yoke assembly into Slot 1 on the system board*

Figure 5-7 *Installing the Pentium II processor into the retention yoke assembly*

You can install the Pentium II only one way, but with a PGA-packaged processor, it is possible to install it backwards, damaging the processor's pins. When installing a PGA-packaged processor, ensure that the # 1 pin in the processor's PGA aligns with the # 1 pin-socket in the socket's PGA by following several steps.

First, ensure that the ZIF handle is in the upright position and is ready to accept the processor, thus reducing the insertion force to zero. Next, match the corner of the processor that has a 45-degree chamfer with a white dot on the top surface (indicating # 1 pin) with the corner of the socket PGA that contains one less pin-socket (indicating # 1 pin-socket). Figure 5-8 shows a Classic Pentium; the lower pointer indicates the corner with the # 1 pin and the upper pointer indicates the raised ZIF handle, which reduces the processor insertion force to zero.

Several A+ Core exam questions address 486DX4 installation. You should recognize that the power requirement for the 486DX is 3.3 volts rather than 5 volts (as with the other 486 CPUs). The 486DX and other CPUs will fail if they are over-powered by only a few volts. The 486 also can be installed backwards in its socket, and it will fail if installed improperly.

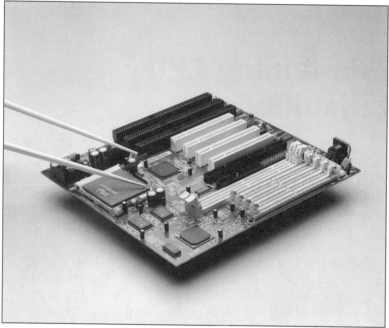

Figure 5-8 *The Classic Pentium. Note the # 1 pin mark on the corner edge and the ZIF handle in the raised position, reducing the processor insertion force to zero.*

True or False?

1. Socket 6 is a popular Classic Pentium socket.
2. The speed range of the Pentium Pro is 150 to 233MHz.
3. The 486 has a 32-bit data bus width and a 32-bit address bus width.

Answers: *1. False 2. False 3. True*

Maintaining CPU Reliability

CPUs must be adequately cooled to maintain longevity. The two types of CPU cooling methods are heat sinks and cooling fans. Heat sinks are used on some pre-Pentium processors. They are metal-finned plates (usually aluminum) that add surface area to the top of the chip, radiating heat away from the CPU. Cooling fans are mounted either directly on top of PGA packages or on the side of the SEC cartridges. The leading cause of CPU problems is failure of the cooling fan.

When installed on the ATX system board, the Pentium II processor is also located near the power supply fan, providing an additional supply of cooling air over the processor's SEC cartridge. Figure 5-9 depicts the cooling fan mounted on the side of the Pentium II SEC cartridge.

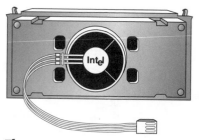

Figure 5-9 *A cooling fan mounted on the side of the Pentium II SEC cartridge*

 There is an A+ Core exam question on the possible cause of a CPU problem. Select the answer that contains a reference to a cooling fan failure.

Have You Mastered?

Now it's time to review the concepts in this chapter and apply your knowledge. These questions test your mastery of the material covered in this chapter.

1. Processors with MMX capability enhance which of the following:

- ☐ A. Media mix execution
- ☐ B. Hard disk data transfer
- ☐ C. Floppy disk data transfer
- ☐ D. Multimedia capability

The correct answer is **D.** MMX is an acronym for MultiMedia Extensions and it is often associated with the Intel processor, Pentium with MMX Technology. The MMX feature in the Pentium adds 57 multimedia-specific instructions to the instruction set, and it increases the L1 cache memory from 16K to 32K — a 15 percent increase in speed compared with the Classic Pentium. Refer to Table 5-1, "Summary of Intel CPU Specifications and Features" and "The Microprocessor Marketplace" section for more information.

2. How much integrated L1 cache memory do Pentium II processors have?

- ☐ A. 512K
- ☐ B. 256K
- ☐ C. 32K
- ☐ D. 64K

The correct answer is **C**. Pentium II processors contain 32K of internal L1 cache memory. Refer to Table 5-1, "Summary of Intel CPU Specifications and Features," for more information.

3. What are the respective data bus and address bus widths of the Pentium II processors?

    ☐ A. 16-bit and 64-bit
    ☐ B. 32-bit and 32-bit
    ☐ C. 64-bit and 36-bit
    ☐ D. 64-bit and 32-bit

The correct answer is **C**. The Pentium II has a data bus width of 64-bits and an address bus width of 36-bits. Refer to the "The Microprocessor Marketplace" section and Table 5-1, "Summary of Intel CPU Specifications and Features," for more information.

4. What are the respective data bus and address bus widths of the Intel 486 processors?

    ☐ A. 16-bit and 32-bit
    ☐ B. 32-bit and 32-bit
    ☐ C. 64-bit and 36-bit
    ☐ D. 64-bit and 32-bit

The correct answer is **B**. Intel 80486 processors have a data bus width of 32-bits and an address bus width of 32-bits. Refer to Table 5-1, "Summary of Intel CPU Specifications and Features" for more information.

5. What are the respective clock and system bus speeds of Pentiums with MMX Technology?

    ☐ A. 150MHz and 66MHz
    ☐ B. 266MHz and 66MHz
    ☐ C. 200MHz and 100MHz
    ☐ D. 266MHz and 100MHz

The correct answer is **B.** Pentium processors with MMX Technology have 166, 200, 233, and 266MHz speeds. The system bus speed is 66MHz. Refer to Table 5-1, "Summary of Intel CPU Specifications and Features," for more information.

6. Which processor uses the 237 pin-socket CPU socket 3?

- ☐ A. Pentium Pro
- ☐ B. 80386
- ☐ C. 80486
- ☐ D. Pentium II

The correct answer is **C.** Intel 80486 processors use the 237 pin-socket CPU Socket 3. Refer to the "Identifying CPU Sockets and Slots" section for more information.

7. What is the physical size of the circuits used in Pentium II 100MHz bus processors?

- ☐ A. 0.35 micron
- ☐ B. 0.25 micron
- ☐ C. 0.18 micron
- ☐ D. 0.46 mm

The correct answer is **B.** A Pentium II 100MHz bus processor uses circuits that are 0.25 microns, whereas other Pentium and Pentium II processors use 0.35- micron circuit sizes. Refer to the "Understanding Features of the Pentium II" section for more information.

8. Which CPU socket or slot supports Pentium Pro processors?

- ☐ A. Socket 8
- ☐ B. Slot 1
- ☐ C. Socket 7
- ☐ D. Slot 5

The correct answer is **A.** CPU Socket 8 with a 387 pin-socket array supports the Pentium Pro processors. Refer to the "Identifying CPU Sockets and Slots" section for more information.

9. **Which processor operates with an L2 cache speed that is one-half the processor's speed?**

      ☐ A. Classic Pentium
      ☐ B. Pentium Pro
      ☐ C. Pentium II 66MHz bus
      ☐ D. Pentium II 100MHz bus

The correct answer is **D.** A Pentium II 100MHz bus operates with an L2 cache speed of one-half the processor's speed. The other processors operate with an L2 cache speed of 66MHz. Refer to the "Understanding Features of the Pentium II" section for more information.

10. **What are the available sizes of L2 cache memory for a Pentium Pro processor?**

      ☐ A. 128K and 256KB
      ☐ B. 256K and 512KB
      ☐ C. 512K and 1.5MB
      ☐ D. 128K and 512KB

The correct answer is **B.** Available sizes of L2 cache memory for a Pentium Pro processor include 256K, 512K, and 1MB. Refer to Table 5-1, "Summary of Intel CPU Specifications and Features," for more information.

RAM and Other Memory Devices

THIS CHAPTER EXPLORES the computer's main memory, random-access memory (RAM), which works hand-in-hand with the central processing unit (CPU). The chapter covers basic RAM technology, physical packaging, and logical configurations. This chapter also presents information on other system memory devices to prepare you for A+ Core exam questions regarding read-only memory (ROM), basic input/output system (BIOS), and cache memory.

Exam Material in This Chapter

Based on the Official Objectives

- Identify basic terms, concepts, and functions of system memory
- Identify locations and physical characteristics of RAM and ROM
- Know how to service RAM and ROM

Based on the Author's Experience

- Understand the differences between RAM and ROM
- Anticipate questions regarding the physical characteristics of dual inline memory modules (DIMMs) and single inline memory modules (SIMMs)
- Prepare to calculate memory capacities based on SIMM format specifications
- Expect questions on parity versus non-parity memory chip designs and error messages
- Be able to identify the different types of dynamic RAM (DRAM) and static ram (SRAM) technologies
- Anticipate questions on the ROM BIOS
- Be prepared to answer questions concerning cache memory
- Expect questions addressing logical memory configurations (also called the *MS-DOS memory map*)
- Know how to install RAM into memory banks on the system board

Are You Prepared?

Test your knowledge with the following questions. Then you'll know if you're prepared for the material in this chapter or if you should review problem areas.

1. **If a memory bank connector slot has 30 pin-sockets (edge connector pad-slots), the RAM is which memory module type?**

   - ☐ A. DIPP
   - ☐ B. DIMM
   - ☐ C. SIMM
   - ☐ D. GPA

2. **A defective memory module can cause which of the following on-screen error messages?**

   - ☐ A. ROM error
   - ☐ B. Parity error
   - ☐ C. SIMM error
   - ☐ D. DIMM error

3. **ROM BIOS contains which of the following programs? (Choose all that apply.)**

   - ☐ A. POST
   - ☐ B. System Setup program
   - ☐ C. The computer's operating system
   - ☐ D. CMOS

Answers:

1. C   *A SIMM contains either 30 or 72 pins, whereas a DIMM has 168 pins. The other two answers have no meaning regarding memory modules. See the "Identifying Main Memory Modules" section.*

2. B   *A parity error message indicates that the data held in RAM is corrupted, whereas the other error messages are invalid. Refer to the "Understanding Parity Error Checking" section.*

3. A and B

     POST and System Setup programs are part of the BIOS encoded on the ROM chip. The OS resides in RAM during the computer's operation and CMOS is on the RTC chip. See the "Comparing Random-Access Memory and Read-only Memory" section.

Comparing Random-Access Memory and Read-only Memory

The two primary types of computer memory are random-access memory (RAM) and read-only memory (ROM). RAM, or main memory, is a relatively fast, volatile semiconductor storage media that requires constant power to maintain its information. The CPU uses RAM to temporarily store and retrieve data, calculation results, and operating system and application program instructions. Other system hardware devices also use RAM to temporarily store and retrieve information. RAM is read/write data storage.

ROM is a slower, non-volatile storage media that requires no power to retain its read-only software program instructions, the system basic input/output system (BIOS). The BIOS runs the power-on self-test (POST), initiates the loading of the operating system during the computer's boot sequence, runs the System Setup program for user access to device settings in the Complimentary Metal-Oxide Semiconductor (CMOS), and enables communication between the CPU and system hardware devices during operation.

Because ROM is much slower than RAM, RAM often *shadows* ROM. ROM *shadowing* means that part of the BIOS program is copied from ROM into RAM during the boot sequence to reduce the startup time.

There is an A+ Core exam question on which term is used to describe copying part of BIOS from ROM BIOS into RAM to improve startup performance. The correct answer is *shadowing*.

For increased RAM capacity and ease of RAM upgrade and replacement, modern RAM is packaged in modules or small circuit boards and installed in memory banks or groups of vertical slot connectors mounted on the system board. The ROM BIOS chip, on the other hand, is mounted in either a chip carrier or soldered directly to the system board. Flash BIOS, which can be updated using software, is an example of a ROM BIOS chip soldered to the system board.

RAM versus ROM

For the A+ Core exam, you should know that RAM is relatively fast, volatile memory that requires constant power to maintain its data. In contrast, ROM is slower, non-volatile memory that needs no power to retain its software program, called BIOS. RAM is read/write data storage, whereas ROM is read-only data storage. You should also know that Flash BIOS can be upgraded using software rather than chip replacement.

Understanding Dynamic RAM

The computer's main memory or RAM uses a semiconductor memory technology called dynamic RAM (DRAM). DRAM is slower than other memory technologies, such as the static RAM (SRAM) used in cache memory, but DRAM is less expensive than faster memory types. The term dynamic in DRAM means that the memory cells must be constantly refreshed every 2 to 40 milliseconds (depending on the DRAM technology) to retain their data. In contrast, SRAM is a self-refreshing memory technology; this means that it does not depend on an external circuit for a source of cell refreshment power like DRAM.

DRAM Technologies

As DRAM technology matured over the last 20 years, RAM access time has been reduced from 120 nanoseconds (a nanosecond is a billionth of a second) to 10 nanoseconds or less. The speed of the system memory bus also has increased from 66MHz (number of timing pulses per second) to 100MHz.

The evolution in RAM performance began with fast-page mode (FPM) RAM. Today, high performance and specialized DRAM technologies, such as synchronous dynamic RAM (SDRAM) and Video RAM

(VRAM) are available in the marketplace. The performance characteristics of various DRAM technologies are as follows:

- **Fast-page mode (FPM) RAM** is an example of early DRAM technology. Although FPM RAM is not used in today's computers because of its relatively slow access time (approximately 120 nanoseconds), it is still supported in the after-sale marketplace.

- **Extended data out (EDO) RAM** permits a data access cycle to begin before the previous cycle has been completed. EDO RAM is only 10 to 20 percent faster than FPM RAM, but it is currently the most popular type of DRAM technology.

- **Burst EDO (BEDO) RAM** combines EDO DRAM with bursting and pipelining technologies. Bursting technology enables large blocks of data to be sent and processed as uninterrupted *bursts* of smaller data units. Pipelining technology collects data requests within the data *bursts* so that the execution requests are almost instantaneous. BEDO RAM access time is approximately 10 nanoseconds, rivaling that of SDRAM. However, BEDO RAM cannot operate over 66MHz and has little industry support.

- **Synchronous dynamic RAM (SDRAM)** is the new standard for main memory because it has the same capabilities as BEDO RAM and uses the 100MHz system bus speed. It also is directly synchronized with the system clock pulse rate to maximize refresh rate and access speed. Additionally, SDRAM technology permits two pages of memory to be opened simultaneously. (The PC-100 SDRAM is used by the Pentium II with a 100MHz processor bus and the Pentium III.)

A+ Core exam questions and answer choices use various acronyms instead of complete terms to describe memory devices. You should know what the acronyms stand for, as well as the information in this list of DRAM technologies.

- **RAMBus (RDRAM)** is a DRAM technology currently being developed by Intel. It removes latency, or the time to access RAM, by changing the memory bus to a separate communication channel for an even faster RAM technology compared with SDRAM.

- **Video RAM (VRAM)** is a special DRAM technology designed specifically to enhance video performance. VRAM is generally located on video accelerator cards and used to store the pixel values of a graphics display while the video controller reads continuously from the memory to refresh the display. VRAM significantly increases video performance compared with most other DRAM types, but it is more expensive.

- **Windows Accelerator RAM (WRAM)** is a special DRAM technology designed specifically to improve graphics performance like VRAM does, but WRAM offers a larger bandwidth than VRAM.

Characteristics of DRAM Technology

Four or five A+ Core exam questions are on comparing various DRAM characteristics. At a minimum, you should know the following DRAM facts:

- DRAM is slower but less expensive than SRAM.

- DRAM requires refreshment every 2 to 40 milliseconds, depending on the type of DRAM technology. SRAM does not require external refreshment.

- Although they are similar, SDRAM has a faster access time and refresh rate than BEDO RAM because it uses the 100MHz memory bus synchronized pulse rate.

- Bursting technology enables uninterrupted *bursts* of small data units.

- Pipelining technology collects data requests within the *bursts* so execution requests are almost instantaneous.
- VRAM and WRAM are used for graphics enhancement, and they are faster than many other DRAM types but more expensive.

DRAM Packaging

DRAM is packaged in three forms: dual in-line package (DIP), small outline j-lead (SOJ), and thin, small outline package (TSOP).

Older DIP-packaged DRAM chips are through-hole components, which means that their pins, or feet, extend through holes in the printed circuit board (PCB), and are soldered in place for electrical and mechanical retention. DIP DRAM chips can also be installed in system board-mounted chip carriers for upgrade and replacement ease.

Modern SOJ and TSOP DRAM chips are surface-mount components soldered to small circuit boards called *memory modules*. The memory modules are then installed in vertical memory banks on the system board.

Identifying Main Memory Modules

Main memory modules are small circuit boards that contain individual surface-mounted SOJ or TSOP DRAM chips. The modules are categorized as either single inline memory modules (SIMMs) or dual inline memory modules (DIMMS).

Single Inline Memory Modules

Single inline memory module (SIMM) circuit boards have either 30-pin gold or 72-pin tin/lead edge connectors, and have memory capacities between 256K and 32MB. 30-pin SIMM configurations were designed to support older 8-bit CPUs, such as the Intel 8088. However, a minimum of four 30-pin SIMMs can also be used to support 32-bit CPUs, such as the 80486. One or more 72-pin SIMM can be used to support a 32-bit processor, and two or more SIMMs, arranged in pairs, can be used to support 64-data bit CPUs, such as the Pentium. The dimensions of 30-pin and 72-pin SIMMs are 3.5-inches long and 4.25-inches long, respectively. SIMMs require 5.0 volts of power.

Dual Inline Memory Modules

Dual inline memory module (DIMM) circuit boards have 168-pin gold connectors with individual DRAM chips mounted on both sides that are electrically interconnected. DIMMs have memory capacities between 8MB and 256MB. One or more DIMM can support 64-data bit processors, such as the Pentiums. DIMMs are 5.25-inches long and require either 3.3 volts or 5.0 volts of power. Figure 6-1 shows a 30-pin SIMM, 72-pin SIMM, and 168-pin DIMM.

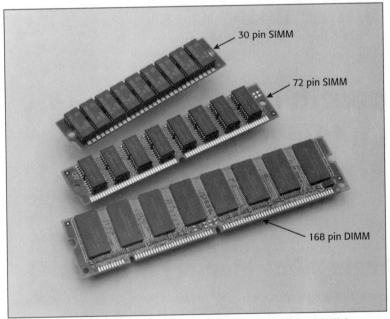

Figure 6-1 *A 30-pin SIMM, 72-pin SIMM, and 168-pin DIMM*

Expect two A+ Core exam questions on SIMM and DIMM pin count: 30-pin SIMM, 72-pin SIMM, and 168-pin DIMM.

Installing Main Memory Modules

SIMMs and DIMMs are usually installed vertically in memory banks on the system board. Most Baby AT and ATX system boards contain both SIMM and DIMM memory banks. However, SIMMs and DIMMs should never be installed simultaneously because the operating system will not accurately detect the amount of available memory, and the data transfer rate between the RAM and CPU will be reduced significantly.

Figure 6-2 depicts SIMM and DIMM memory banks on a Baby AT system board. Note that the DIMM memory bank connector slots are longer than the SIMM connector slots.

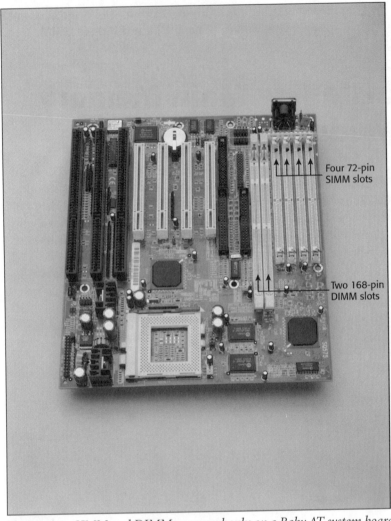

Four 72-pin
SIMM slots

Two 168-pin
DIMM slots

Figure 6-2 *SIMM and DIMM memory banks on a Baby AT system board*

To install a SIMM into a memory bank, follow these steps:

1. Match pin 1 of the SIMM to socket 1 in the memory bank slot by aligning the module cutout (shown in Figure 6-3) with the corresponding slot shoulder. The SIMM should also be inserted into the slot at a 45-degree angle, as shown in Figure 6-4.

2. Firmly swing the SIMM into the vertical position until the clips on each side click into place.

Figure 6-3 *The SIMM cutout ensures correct installation into memory bank slot*

Figure 6-4 *An initial insertion of a SIMM at a 45-degree angle*

SIMMs must be installed in pairs if they support 64-data bit CPUs, such as the Pentiums. One or more DIMM can be installed to support the Pentiums.

To install a DIMM into a memory bank slot, follow these steps:

1. Match pin 1 of the DIMM to socket 1 of the memory bank slot by aligning the module cutouts (as depicted in Figure 6-5) with the corresponding slot shoulders. The DIMM should also be inserted into the slot at a 45-degree angle, as shown in Figure 6-6.

2. Firmly swing the DIMM into the vertical position and lock the side latches to secure the DIMM in the slot.

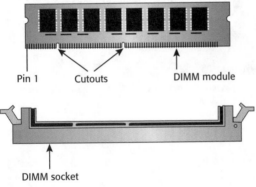

Figure 6-5 *The DIMM cutouts ensure correct installation into memory bank slot*

Figure 6-6 *An initial insertion of a DIMM at a 45-degree angle*

True or False?

1. ROM is faster than RAM.

2. DIMMs contain 72-pin edge connectors.

3. EDO RAM is faster than FPM RAM.

Answers: *1. False   2. False   3. True*

Understanding Parity Error Checking

RAM parity is a process that stores one parity bit for every eight bits of stored data. With odd parity, the parity bit is forced to 1 (or turned on) if its corresponding byte of data contains an even number of 1s. If the byte contains an odd number of 1s, the parity bit is forced to 0 (or turned off). (The opposite process occurs in even parity.) The data byte plus the parity bit is then written to the RAM. Before the data byte is sent to the CPU, the parity circuit inspects the data byte to ensure the parity is the same parity as when it entered RAM. Validated data bytes have their parity bits stripped from the data, and the data is sent on to the CPU. A parity error message is posted on the computer's screen if the parity is invalid.

The value of RAM parity is limited because even though the parity circuit detects errors, it cannot perform corrections. Additionally, because of price pressures and improved RAM quality, data checking is generally not used in current memory designs.

There is an A+ Core exam question on the cause of parity errors. The correct answer is that repeated on-screen parity errors are caused by faulty RAM.

Calculating Memory Capacities

The memory capacity of a SIMM is specified in terms of its depth and width format and whether or not it supports parity. To determine the module's memory capacity, divide the specified second term representing width by either eight (non-parity) bits or nine (parity) bits to convert it to bytes, and then multiply the calculated number of bytes by the first number, which is the depth in MB. For example, an 8M × 32, 72-pin SIMM is a 32MB non-parity memory module. Another example is that a parity SIMM using an 8M × 36, 72-pin SIMM format has a 32MB capacity. Table 6-1 presents examples of various SIMM formats and capacities.

Table 6-1 SIMM Formats and Capacities

SIMM Type	Parity/ Non-Parity	SIMM Format	SIMM Capacity
30-pin	Parity	1M X 9	1MB
30-pin	Parity	4M X 9	4MB
30-pin	Non-Parity	1M X 8	1MB
30-pin	Non-Parity	4M X 8	4MB
72-pin	Parity	4M X 36	16MB
72-pin	Parity	8M X 36	32MB
72-pin	Non-Parity	4M X 32	16MB
72-pin	Non-Parity	8M X 32	32MB

To answer the A+ Core question on DIMM memory capacity, divide the specified second term representing width by either eight (non-parity) bits or nine (parity) bits to convert it to bytes, and then multiply the calculated number of bytes by the first number, which is the depth in MB. For example, a 4M × 32, 72-pin SIMM is a 16MB non-parity memory module.

Configuring Logical RAM

The computer's operating system configures the physical RAM into specific memory divisions called *logical RAM areas* (also called the *MS-DOS memory map*). It automatically configures physical RAM and manages logical RAM by loading the HIMEM.SYS and EMM386.EXE programs in the CONFIG.SYS startup file into RAM during computer boot. Table 6-2 summarizes the logical RAM areas.

Table 6-2 Summary of Logical Memory Areas

RAM Area	Area Location	Remarks
Conventional memory	First 640K	Used by DOS programs, device drivers, and buffers
Upper memory area	From 640K to 1MB	Stores video and other adapter RAM and ROM, system BIOS (ROM shadowing), system devices, and buffers
Extended memory area (XMA)	After 1MB up to 4GB	Used for Windows and Windows-based programs
High memory area (HMA)	First 64K of XMA	Stores DOS when DOS=HIGH command is in the CONFIG.SYS file
Expanded memory (EMS)	After XMA	Eases conventional memory by accepting its overload

When Microsoft and IBM engineers built the first Intel 8088 processor-based PC in 1980, they divided 1MB of physical RAM into logical areas using the hexadecimal addressing system (letters A through F represent the numbers 10 through 15). They designated the first 640K block of addresses as conventional memory and identified the remaining 384K of addresses as upper memory. The addressing within each block was further allocated or segregated for use by specific programs, devices, and other software routines.

When the 80286 was introduced, an additional 15MB of addresses were allocated and divided into high memory, extended memory, and expanded memory. The logical memory address limit increased to 4GB with the advent of the Pentium processor.

MS-DOS memory device drivers HIMEM.SYS and EMM386.EXE, which are in the CONFIG.SYS startup file and loaded into RAM during boot, manage the mapped memory areas. Figure 6-7 illustrates the MS-DOS memory map.

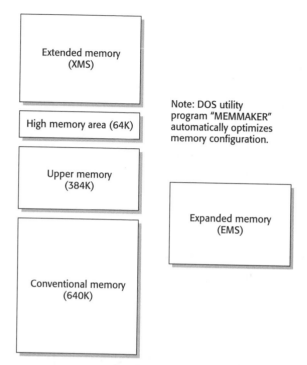

Note: DOS utility program "MEMMAKER" automatically optimizes memory configuration.

Figure 6-7 *An MS-DOS memory map*

Logical Memory Areas

Four A+ Core exam questions focus on identifying the logical memory areas. To prepare for these questions, memorize the following:

- Conventional memory (first 640K)
- Upper memory area (384K after conventional memory to 1MB)
- Extended memory area (after upper memory to 4GB limit)
- High memory area (first 64K of extended memory)
- Expanded memory (supports conventional memory)

Understanding Cache Memory

Cache is a special memory subsystem in which frequently used data is duplicated for quick access. Level 1 cache (also called L1 cache or CPU on-board cache) memory is located inside the CPU. Level 2 cache (also called L2 cache) memory is either a single static RAM (SRAM) chip or multiple SRAM chips, usually mounted on the system board between the CPU and RAM. Pentium Pro and Celeron processors, however, have L2 cache memory integrated in their pin grid array (PGA) packages.

On Pentium II and Pentium III processors, a single 512K L2 cache memory chip is mounted on a small circuit board with the Intel P6 processor inside the processor's single-edge-contact (SEC) cartridge.

Cache memory is approximately five times faster than system RAM is. The CPU searches first for data first in the L1 cache, then the L2 cache, and finally in the RAM.

The Characteristics of Cache Memory

You should know that cache memory (SRAM technology) is approximately five times faster than system RAM (DRAM technology). Additionally, you should know that the CPU searches first for data in the L1 cache, then the L2 cache, and finally in the RAM.

Have You Mastered?

Now it's time to review the concepts in this chapter and apply your knowledge. These questions test your mastery of the material covered in this chapter.

1. The logical memory area after 1MB of RAM is called:

- ☐ A. Upper memory area
- ☐ B. Conventional memory
- ☐ C. Extended memory
- ☐ D. Expanded memory

The correct answer is **C.** Extended memory is the area following 1MB of RAM. Refer to the "Configuring Logical RAM" section for more information.

2. Which DRAM technology is used with the Pentium II 100MHz bus processor?

- ☐ A. BDO RAM
- ☐ B. SDRAM
- ☐ C. VRAM
- ☐ D. EDO RAM

The correct answer is **B.** SDRAM is the only DRAM technology that can operate at the 100MHz-memory bus speed, supporting the newest Pentium II and Pentium III processors. Refer to the "Understanding Dynamic RAM" section for more information.

3. Which memory module has 30 pins?

☐ A. DIMM
☐ B. DRAM
☐ C. SRAM
☐ D. SIMM

The correct answer is **D.** A SIMM contains either 30 pins or 72 pins. Refer to the "Identifying Main Memory Modules" section for more information.

4. The first 640K logical area of RAM is called:

☐ A. Expanded memory
☐ B. Upper memory
☐ C. Conventional memory
☐ D. Extended memory

The correct answer is **C.** Conventional memory is the first 640K of memory. Refer to the "Configuring Logical RAM" section for more information.

5. How many pins (edge connector pads) are on a DIMM?

☐ A. 128
☐ B. 72
☐ C. 168
☐ D. 148

The correct answer is **A.** A DIMM has 168 pins or edge connector pads. Refer to the "Identifying Main Memory Modules" section for more information.

6. What is the minimum number of 72-pin SIMMs required for a Pentium processor?

☐ A. two
☐ B. one
☐ C. four
☐ D. eight

The correct answer is **A.** A minimum of two 72-pin (32-bit) SIMMs are required to support the Pentium (64-data bit) processor. Refer to the "Installing Main Memory Modules" section for more information.

7. Which problem symptom would POST not identify?

- ☐ A. Faulty keyboard
- ☐ B. Bad memory location
- ☐ C. Faulty hard drive
- ☐ D. RAM failing at high temperature

The correct answer is **D.** POST tests the hardware devices only during a cold boot. Refer to the "Comparing Random-Access Memory and Read-only Memory" section.

8. Which 72-pin SIMM format indicates a 16MB memory capacity without parity?

- ☐ A. 4M X 36
- ☐ B. 4M X 32
- ☐ C. 16M X 1
- ☐ D. 4M X 4

The correct answer is **B.** 16MB is calculated from the 4M × 32 format by dividing the second term by eight and multiplying the result by the first term. Refer to the "Calculating Memory Capacities" section for more information.

9. Which memory chip type does not require power to retain its data?

- ☐ A. BIOS
- ☐ B. CMOS
- ☐ C. RAM
- ☐ D. ROM

The correct answer is **D.** Unlike RAM, ROM does not require power to maintain its data. Refer to the "Comparing Random-Access Memory and Read-only Memory" section for more information.

10. Which term describes the process of copying part of BIOS into RAM?

☐ A. Flash BIOS
☐ B. ROM shadowing
☐ C. PnP BIOS
☐ D. BIOS duplicating

The correct answer is **B.** ROM shadowing describes the process of copying part of the BIOS into RAM. Refer to the "Comparing Random-Access Memory and Read-only Memory" section for more information.

Disk Storage Devices

THIS CHAPTER ADDRESSES disk storage devices, including hard disk drives (HDDs) and floppy disk drives (FDDs). It prepares you for A+ Core exam questions on hard disk drive construction, data storage organization, performance, and system interface standards. After completing this chapter, you also will be able to answer questions on how to install, configure, partition, and format disk drives.

Exam Material in This Chapter

Based on the Official Objectives

- Identify basic terms, concepts, and functions of disk storage devices
- Identify proper procedures for installing and configuring disk storage devices
- Know how to service disk storage devices

Based on the Author's Experience

- Understand how HDDs are constructed
- Expect questions on HDD file structure and data organization
- Know how to install, configure, partition, and format HDDs
- Understand HDD seek time and data transfer rate differences
- Prepare to answer questions concerning File Allocation Table (FAT) and FAT32
- Anticipate questions regarding Integrated Drive Electronics (IDE), Enhanced IDE (EIDE), and Small Computer System Interface (SCSI) HDD system interfaces
- Learn how to configure master and slave HDDs during installation
- Expect questions addressing FDDs and diskette data capacities

Are You Prepared?

1. **Which of the following statements is true with regard to HDD data structure?**

   - ☐ A. A cluster is a group of tracks.
   - ☐ B. A cluster is a group of cylinders.
   - ☐ C. A cluster is a group of sectors.
   - ☐ D. A cluster is a group of segments.

2. **Which HDD specification addresses the amount of data a HDD and controller can send to the operating system in one second?**

   - ☐ A. Data transfer rate
   - ☐ B. Data transport speed
   - ☐ C. Data access time
   - ☐ D. Data latency speed

3. **What is the maximum number of devices the primary channel of the EIDE HDD system interface standard can support?**

   - ☐ A. One
   - ☐ B. Two
   - ☐ C. Three
   - ☐ D. Four

Answers:

1. C   *A cluster is a group of sectors that the operating system treats as one entity for data storage purposes. See the "Formatting Disks" section.*

2. A   *Data transfer rate defines the amount of data that a HDD and controller can send to the operating system in one second. See the "HDD Performance" section.*

3. B   *The primary EIDE interface channel supports one master device and one slave device. The secondary channel also supports two IDE devices. See the "EIDE Interface Standard" section.*

Understanding Disk Storage Devices

Hard disk and floppy disk drives are considered long-term, non-volatile data storage devices because they permanently store data without refreshment and continuous applied power. They use a magnetic data storage technology that is similar to what tape recorders use to store large volumes of data. In contrast, RAM is short-term, volatile data storage that uses semiconductor technology requiring continuous power.

 Several A+ Core exam questions ask about contrasting data storage device technologies. Remember that disk drives are long-term, non-volatile data storage devices. RAM, on the other hand, is short-term, volatile data storage.

Since hard disk drives (HDDs) were first introduced in the early 1980s, their data storage capacities have increased dramatically from 20MB (megabytes) to tens of GBs (gigabytes). Simultaneously, both the size of HDDs and the cost per storage unit have been significantly reduced. Figure 7-1 illustrates HDD data capacity increases in relation to size reductions.

HDDs are electromechanical devices that typically contain from two to eight rigid disks (also called *platters*) that are coated with a thin film of magnetically sensitive material. The platters are assembled on a spindle (also called *a hub*), and a spindle motor rotates the assembly at high speeds. Read/write heads record and retrieve binary data by sensing and changing the magnetic field polarity of the platter's surface material.

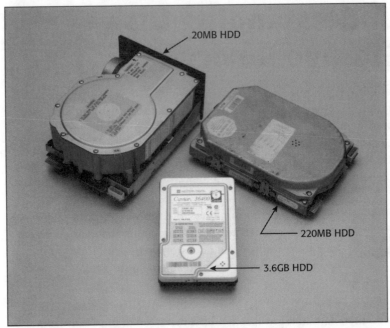

Figure 7-1 *HDD data capacity increases and correlating size reductions*

The computer's operating system identifies a single HDD as drive C:. If drive C: is partitioned or if additional drives are installed, the new partitions or drives are designated drives D:, E:, F:, and so forth.

Floppy disk drives (FDDs) work much like HDDs do, except that FDDs use only a single removable disk to store the data. Today's FDDs store and retrieve data on 3.5-inch floppy disks (also called diskettes) that typically have 1.44MB, 120MB, or 200MB data capacities; these disks are used to install programs, transfer files, and back up data.

The computer's operating system identifies a single FDD as drive A:. If a second FDD is installed, it is designated drive B:.

Formatting Disks

Because disks hold millions or even billions of binary data bits, a means of data organization must be employed to rapidly locate a particular sequence of bits composing a data or program file. The process for creating data organization is called *formatting*. Formatting prepares hard disks and floppy disks for data storage and retrieval by organizing their storage space into a collection of *compartments*. The data storage compartments, or sectors, can then be accessed for data storage and retrieval by the operating system, which uses a directory or a file allocation table to *look up* file locations or addresses on a disk. There are two types of formatting: physical and logical.

Physical Formatting

The disk manufacturer usually performs the physical (also called *low-level* or *absolute*) formatting of disks. Physical formatting electrically creates a layout of organized data storage areas or physical elements in the disk's surface material, defining the way in which data is physically recorded and retrieved. It divides the disk into tracks and sectors, as depicted in Figure 7-2.

- Tracks are numerous concentric rings emanating from the center of the disk. Each disk side, or surface (also called *the head*), and each disk, or platter, in the drive contains tracks similar to those of a vinyl record, except that the tracks are not spiral; they are evenly spaced. These tracks are identified by numbers, beginning with track zero at the outer edge.

- Sectors divide each track into individual segments, which are used to store a fixed amount of data. Sectors are usually formatted to contain up to 512 bytes (8 bits per byte) of data.

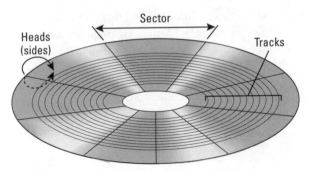

Figure 7-2 *A physically formatted disk*

To address disk file locations, the operating system uses the tracks and sectors to describe the cylinders and clusters in hard disks, and the clusters in floppy disks.

- Unique to hard disk drives, cylinders are groups of tracks vertically aligned through multiple disk platter heads at the same track number. They enable the operating system to read and write data to each platter head on the same track, reducing the need to move the read/write heads.

- Clusters are a fixed number of sectors, which are based on the disk's volume storage capacity and the type of file system. The operating system typically uses a minimum of one cluster to store one file.

 To answer A+ Core exam questions regarding disk physical formats, memorize the definitions of disk tracks, sectors, cylinders, and clusters.

Logical Formatting

After they have been physically formatted (and after the hard disk has been partitioned with a primary DOS partition), disks must be logically formatted. Logical formatting can be done with a disk management utility program, such as DOS's FORMAT. The FORMAT program essentially prepares the disk to receive data and then creates the following files and areas on track zero of the disk:

- The DOS file system called File Allocation Table (FAT)
- The DOS Root Directory
- The DOS Boot Record

The following are common operating system file systems:

- The FAT, or FAT16, file system can be used by DOS, Windows 3.*x*, Windows 95, Windows NT, and OS/2. FAT is based on a 16-bit file allocation system and can support hard disk volumes up to 2GB.

- The FAT32 file system can be used by Windows 95 (Version 4.00.950B only), Windows 98, and Windows 2000. FAT32 is based on a 32-bit file allocation table and can support volumes up to 2TB (terabytes). FAT32 also is more efficient than FAT16 because it uses smaller cluster sizes. For example, its cluster size is 4K at a 2GB volume compared with 32K for FAT16.

- The Virtual FAT (VFAT) 32-bit file system overlays FAT, acting as a virtual interface between applications and physical FAT. It provides long filenames up to 255 characters and file pathnames up to 260 characters.

- The New Technology File System (NTFS) file system is used by Windows NT and Windows 2000. It provides enhanced performance, security, and data loss prevention methods. NTFS is more efficient than either FAT16 or FAT32 because it uses a smaller cluster size (512 bytes at a 2GB capacity volume).

After a disk partition has been logically formatted, the operating system refers to it as a volume.

DOS and Windows File Systems

You should know the following about DOS and Windows file systems:

- DOS uses a File Allocation Table (FAT), or FAT16, file system, which supports volumes up to 2GB.

- Windows 3.*x* uses a FAT16 and Virtual FAT (VFAT) file system, which supports long file names.

- Window 95 uses FAT16, VFAT, and FAT32 (Version 4.00.950B only) file systems. FAT32 supports volumes up to 2TB.

- Windows NT uses New Technology File System (NTFS) and FAT16 file systems.

Also know that FAT32 is more efficient with a cluster size of 4K at a 2GB volume compared with 32K for FAT16.

Partitioning the Hard Disk Drive

Rather than leaving it as one large hard disk drive or a single volume, a physical HDD can be divided into numerous logical drives or separate volumes by a process called *partitioning*. Partitioning increases data storage efficiency by reducing cluster size and increases security by segregating data and program files. Several operating systems also can be installed in one physical drive if it is partitioned. Partitioning can be performed prior to logical formatting using a disk management utility program, such as FDISK, NT Disk Administrator, or the third-party program, Partition Magic.

The two main types of HDD partitions are primary and extended. If FDISK is used to partition the HDD, one primary and one extended DOS partition is created. The primary DOS partition is also called *the active partition* (and is designated drive C: by DOS) because this partition is the one used by DOS to boot the system. The extended partition can be divided into as many as 23 logical drives, which are designated D: through Z: after logical formatting.

If Partition Magic is used to partition the HDD, up to four main partitions can be created as either four primary partitions or three primary partitions and one extended partition. Only one extended partition can be created, and it can contain numerous logical volumes after formatting but contains no operating systems. A different operating system can be installed in each primary partition. Figure 7-3 depicts three primary partitions containing operating systems and one extended partition containing two logical partitions.

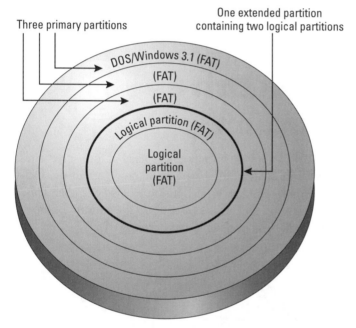

Figure 7-3 *Three primary partitions containing operating systems and one extended partition containing two logical partitions*

FAT16 file systems can support primary partitions up to only 2GB. To use disk space in excess of 2GB, the HDD must be divided into partitions, each smaller than 2GB. FAT32, on the other hand, can support primary partitions up to 8GB.

KNOW THIS — Partitioning the HDD

You should know the following about partitioning HDDs:

- Partitioning is performed after physical formatting but before logical formatting.
- FDISK is the DOS disk management program used to partition.
- A FAT16 file system can support primary partitions up to only 2GB, whereas FAT32 supports 8GB primary partitions.

Hard Disk Drive Construction

The hard disk drive assembly is typically constructed of four subassemblies: disk platters, read/write heads, head positioning mechanism, and spindle motor assembly. They are located inside a sealed chamber. The logic board is mounted on the outside (usually on the bottom) of the assembly. Figure 7-4 illustrates the inside of a typical HDD.

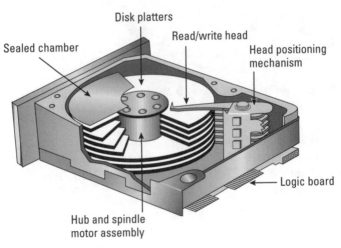

Figure 7-4 *Inside a typical HDD*

Disk Platters

Hard disk drives contain between two and eight rigid disk platters, which are rotated at a constant speed by the spindle motor. The platter rotation speed of current HDDs is typically 5,400, 7,200, or 10,000 revolutions per minute (rpm); better HDD performance is at the higher end of the range. The platters are usually made from an aluminum alloy or a glass and ceramic composite coated with a thin film of magnetically sensitive material. The platters are lightweight and strong to withstand the high centrifugal forces.

Read/Write Heads

The read head of the read/write head pair retrieves binary data by sensing and then converting the material's magnetic field polarity on the platter's surface to electrical signals. These signals are sent either to the central processing unit (CPU) or to the remote-access memory (RAM) if direct memory access (DMA) is employed. Conversely, the write head of the read/write pair converts electrical signals from the CPU or RAM to changes in the surface material's magnetic field polarity.

HDDs contain one read/write head pair for each platter surface or side (also called *head*). They *float* on a cushion of air several millionths of an inch thick that is generated by the spinning platters. Contact between the read/write heads and the platter's surface results in a *head crash* and often causes a total failure of the HDD.

HDD Head Crash

You should know that a *head crash* occurs if the read/write heads come in contact with the magnetic coating on the disk platter's surface, and this often causes a total failure of the HDD. Head crashes usually result from mechanical failures or physical impact. The HDD assembly should never be disassembled because even a speck of dust lodged between the read/write heads and the platter's surface can damage the sensitive magnetic coating.

Head Positioning Mechanism

Read/write heads are attached to the tips of movable arms that are part of the positioning mechanism, enabling the heads to be positioned over any track on the platters' surfaces. A small, fast voice-coil-actuator-motor rapidly moves the arms of the mechanism, providing HDD assembly miniaturization and fast data access times.

HDD data storage and retrieval subassemblies are much faster than tape recorders because with tape recorders, the tape must be unwound from one spool and wound onto the other spool until the data is located for retrieval by the read head.

TEST TIP Although tape drives hold large quantities of data and are considered true mass storage devices, they are much slower than hard disk drives because of inefficient data storage and inefficient retrieval subassemblies.

Spindle Motor Assemblies

Rotational speed is a major factor in hard disk drive performance and data transfer rates. It governs the speed at which the media passes under the read/write heads and the time it takes the heads to read and write the data. Modern HDDs typically have speeds of 5,400, 7,200, or 10,000 rpm; older HDDs have speeds of 3,600 rpm.

To spin the disk platters at high speeds, a low-profile direct current (DC) motor is built into the hub or spindle in the plane of rotation, reducing the vertical profile (or side dimension) of the HDD. The motor is similar in design to the floppy disk drive motor that spins the single disk.

The spindle motor assembly rotates the disk platters at a constant speed that is precisely controlled by a feedback loop circuit. The circuit uses magnetic or optical sensors to detect the rotational speed of the subassembly and provide a feedback signal to the drive's motor speed control electronics.

Logic Boards

Usually mounted on the bottom of the HDD assembly, the logic board contains the electronic circuits and logic chips that control spindle motor-speed and head-positioning mechanism movement. Integrated Dive Electronics (IDE) or Enhanced IDE (EIDE) HDD interface controllers are integrated into the logic board electronics rather than on an expansion board in an expansion slot on the system board like the original IBM ST-506 PC interface standard.

For the A+ Core exam, remember that IDE stands for Integrated Dive Electronics and that the controller is integrated into the on-board HDD electronics, as opposed to being located on an expansion board like the original IBM ST-506 PC interface standard.

Logic boards also contain either 256K or 512K of cache memory (if cache memory is not located within the HDD assembly), system interface electronics, a 40-pin interface connector, and a 3- or 4-pin power connector.

Hard Disk Drive Performance

HDD performance is measured not only by maximum data storage capacity, but also by several other performance measurements and specifications, including data access time, data access rate, rotational speed, and the amount of onboard cache.

Data Access Time

Data access time is the average elapsed time between an operating system data request and data delivery. It consists of two components:

- **Seek time:** the time required for the read/write head to position over a track to read or write the data

- **Rotational latency period:** the time required for the sector to move under the read/write head

EIDE and SCSI HDDs have typical data access times of less than 10 milliseconds.

Data Transfer Rate

The data transfer rate is the amount of data that an HDD and controller can send to the operating system in one second. The greater the amount of data transferred in one second, the better the overall HDD performance.

Typical data transfer rates of modern HDDs include 40MB/sec for a Wide Ultra SCSI-3 HDD and 33.3MB/sec for an Ultra DMA/33 EIDE HDD.

Rotational Speed

Rotational speed is the number of revolutions that the disk platters spin in one minute. The faster the rotational speed, the more data passes under the read/write head in a set period of time. Typical disk platter rotational speeds are 5,400, 7,200, and 10,000 rpm.

Onboard Cache

Onboard cache (also called *buffer memory*) performs a buffer (short-term data storage) function for data being transferred to and from the HDD. Typical onboard cache capacities are 256K and 512K.

 True or False?

1. FAT32 is based on a 32-bit file allocation table and can support volumes of up to 2TB (terabytes).
2. Sectors typically can contain up to 512 bytes of data.
3. A physical HDD can be partitioned into four extended partitions.

Answers: *1. True   2. True   3. False*

Hard Disk Drive System Interface Standards

Hard disk drive system interface standards are recommendations to manufacturers on how their designs should interface physically and electrically with computer systems. HDD system interface designs were first published in the 1980s and are governed by American National Standards Institute (ANSI) standards.

Two common HDD system interfaces are EIDE and SCSI. EIDE (also called ATA-2/EIDE) is basically an extension of the original IDE (also called ATA/IDE) standard and includes many new features that enhance HDD capability and performance.

SCSI system interfaces have evolved through three major versions, which include SCSI-1, SCSI-2, and SCSI-3. SCSI standards have several advantages over EIDE, such as higher data transfer rates and the capability to support more devices.

EIDE Interface Standard

EIDE extends the original IDE design standard by enabling additional devices to be installed on the I/O expansion bus, by increasing data transfer rates, by increasing data capacities, and by including direct memory access. Specifically, EIDE offers the following enhancements:

- The maximum device support is increased from two to four. This includes up to two EIDE or ATAPI (CD-ROM standard) devices in a master/slave configuration connected to the primary channel on the system board, and up to two devices attached to the secondary channel in a similar master/slave arrangement.

- The data transfer rates is increased to 11.1MB/sec in programmed input/output (PIO) mode 3, 16.6MB/sec in PIO mode 4, and 33.3MB/sec in Ultra direct memory access/33 (DMA/33) mode.

- DMA is incorporated, thus enabling data to be transferred directly to RAM, circumventing the CPU.

- An ATAPI interface is included, which supports CD-ROM and tape drives that connect to an ATA connector.
- Logic Block Addressing (LBA) increases data capacities and data transfer rates by transforming data addresses described by sector, head, and cylinder numbers into physical block addresses for communication with newer Basic Input/Output Systems (BIOSs).

EIDE Interface Standards and Definitions

You should know the following about EIDE interface standards and definitions:

- EIDE is the acronym for Enhanced Integrated Drive Electronics.
- Two devices can be connected in a master/slave arrangement to the primary channel and two devices can be attached in the same configuration to the secondary channel.
- ATAPI is a CD-ROM design standard similar to the EIDE HDD standard.
- PIO is the acronym for Programmed Input/Output.
- LBA is the acronym for Logic Block Addressing.

In addition to performance, EIDE interface design standards also define HDD form and fit, which basically dictates how EIDE HDDs are replaced. To replace EIDE HDDs follow these common steps:

1. Shut down and unplug the computer.
2. Open the system unit case by removing the cover.
3. Discharge the static electricity either by touching an unpainted surface on the case chassis or by wearing an ESD wrist strap.
4. Remove the power and interface ribbon cable connectors (40-pin) and HDD mounting screws.

5. After removing the old HDD, slide the new HDD into the mounting brackets, as shown in Figure 7-5.

6. Reinstall the power and interface ribbon cable, as illustrated in Figure 7-6.

7. Reinstall the mounting screws.

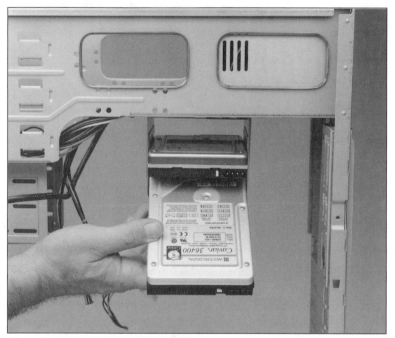

Figure 7-5 *Installing a new HDD into the mounting brackets*

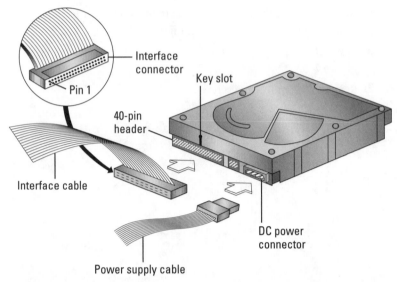

Figure 7-6 *Reconnecting the power supply and interface ribbon cables to the HDD*

HDD Error Messages

You should know about two on-screen error messages that may occur following HDD replacement: Invalid media type and Fixed disk error. The Invalid media type message is usually due to incorrect CMOS settings and the Fixed disk error usually occurs with an unformatted hard disk.

SCSI Interface Standard

SCSI is a totally different system interface than the more popular EIDE. Rather than integrating only the controller on the hard drive as the EIDE interface does, the SCSI is a true standard high-speed parallel hardware interface bus because it supports both internal and external SCSI devices, attached together in a daisy chain, or serial, arrangement. The key features of the SCSI system interface standard are:

- The Narrow SCSI-1 interface standard has an 8-bit (narrow) bus width and supports up to seven attached

SCSI devices (excluding the SCSI host adapter card) at a 5MB/sec data transfer rate.

- The Fast or Ultra SCSI-2 interface standard has an 8-bit (narrow) bus width and supports up to seven attached devices (excluding the SCSI host adapter card) at either a 10MB/sec or a 20MB/sec data transfer rate.

- The Fast Wide or Wide Ultra SCSI-3 has a 16-bit (wide) bus and supports up to 15 attached devices (excluding the SCSI host adapter card) at a 40MB/sec data transfer rate.

- The Wide Ultra 2 SCSI-3 is the newest and fastest SCSI bus at a 80MB/sec data transfer rate and supports up to 15 attached SCSI devices (excluding the SCSI host adapter card).

- Double-ended SCSI chains must be terminated at both ends, but single-ended chains require termination at only the device end because the SCSI host adapter card provides the termination at the other end.

- Narrow SCSI-1 and Fast and Ultra SCSI-2 buses use a 50-pin connector and 50-conductor cable, and Fast Wide or Wide Ultra SCSI-3 buses use a 68-pin connector and 68-conductor cable.

Four or five A+ Core exam questions address the SCSI interface standard. Review the list of SCSI features again and also go back to the "Understanding the Small Computer System Interface Bus" section in Chapter 3. Your extra efforts now will pay off later when you take and pass the exam.

The steps to replace SCSI hard disk drives are similar to those to replace EIDE drives, except that the 50-pin or 68-pin interface ribbon cable is connected to the SCSI host adapter card rather than directly to the system board like the 40-pin EIDE ribbon cable.

Additionally, a SCSI ID must be assigned to the HDD using jumpers or a dual in-line package (DIP) switch block with three rocker arms; this provides eight SCSI ID possibilities with 7 as the highest value. SCSI ID 7 is reserved for the SCSI host adapter card, and an SCSI HDD used to boot the computer should be assigned SCSI ID 0. Also, if a system contains both SCSI and EIDE hard disk drives, the EIDE should be assigned the boot drive using the System Setup program.

Configuring SCSI HDDs

You should know that the SCSI ID range is 0 to 7, with 7 reserved for the SCSI host adapter card and 0 assigned to the boot SCSI HDD. If a system contains both SCSI and EIDE HDDs, the EIDE should be assigned the boot drive using the System Setup program.

Floppy Disk Drive Construction

Although floppy disk drives (FDDs) are relatively simple and inexpensive compared to other system devices, they are important for storing and retrieving data on removable floppy disks or diskettes. HDDs can be used to install programs, transfer files, and back up data.

FDDs are similar to HDDs in design concept and magnetic recording technology except that FDD read/write heads are fixed, or stationary, rather than movable. The floppy disk spins at a constant speed and passes under the heads, which sense or change the polarity of the magnetic coating on the floppy disk's surfaces.

Newer 3.5-inch microfloppy disks are constructed from round disks of polyester film that are coated with ferric oxide particles and encased in a rigid plastic shell that includes a sliding metal cover. Older 5.25-inch floppy disks contain disks of flexible film encased in a flexible plastic jacket. Floppy disk sizes have several data storage capacities, as depicted in Table 7-1.

Table 7-1 Floppy Diskette Data Capacities

Size	Density	Capacity
5.25-inch	Double-density (DD)	360K
5.25-inch	High-density (HD)	1.2MB
3.5-inch	Double-density (DD)	720K
3.5-inch	High-density (HD)	1.44MB
3.5-inch	LS120	120MB

To write-protect a 5.25-inch floppy disk, place a write-protect tab or a piece of tape over the write-protect hole. To write-protect a 3.5-inch microfloppy disk, slide the tab so that the hole is open. Figure 7-7 shows the write-protect holes in the 5.25-inch floppy disk and 3.5-inch microfloppy disk.

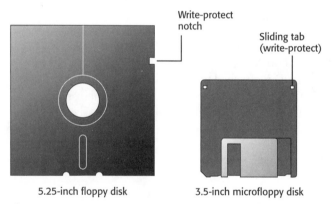

5.25-inch floppy disk   3.5-inch microfloppy disk

Figure 7-7 *Write-protect holes in the 5.25-inch floppy disk and 3.5-inch microfloppy disk*

Replacing Floppy Disk Drives

To replace FDDs, follow these steps:

1. Shut down and unplug the computer.

2. Open the system unit case by removing the unit case cover.

3. Discharge static electricity either by touching an unpainted surface on the case chassis or by wearing a wrist strap.

4. Remove the power and interface system ribbon cable connectors and FDD mounting screws, and slide the old FDD from the mounting bracket.

5. Reinstall the power cable and 34-conductor interface ribbon cable and slide the new FDD into the mounting bracket, as depicted in Figure 7-6.

6. Replace the mounting screws.

FDDs are attached to the computer's FDD controller by a 34-conductor flat ribbon cable, as shown in Figure 7-8. In a single FDD configuration, the FDD is attached to the cable connector after the twist in the cable, or farthest away from the system board connector, and DOS recognizes it as drive A. In a dual FDD configuration, the second FDD is attached to the cable connector before the twist, and DOS identifies it as drive B:.

Figure 7-8 *Installing a new FDD into the mounting brackets. Note that drive A is after the cable twist, or farthest away from the system board connector.*

Memorize the following: HDDs use 40-pin connectors, FDDs use 34-pin connectors, SCSI 1 and SCSI 2 use 50-pin connectors, and SCSI 3 uses 68-pin connectors. This information is worth four correct A+ Core exam answers.

Have You Mastered?

Now it's time to review the concepts in this chapter and apply your knowledge. These questions test your mastery of the material covered in this chapter.

1. Which program is used to partition hard disk drives?

- ☐ A. FDISK
- ☐ B. FORMAT
- ☐ C. System Setup
- ☐ D. DISKSETUP

The correct answer is **A.** The disk management program, FDISK is used to format hard disk drives. Refer to the "Partitioning the Hard Disk Drive" section for more information.

2. A Fast Wide SCSI-3 bus can have up to how many attached devices?

- ☐ A. 8
- ☐ B. 15
- ☐ C. 4
- ☐ D. 7

The correct answer is **B.** Fast Wide or Wide Ultra SCSI-3 buses support up to 15 attached devices, and up to 16 installed devices including the SCSI host adapter card. Refer to the "SCSI Interface Standard" section for more information.

3. How is data protected on a 3.5-inch microfloppy disk?

- ☐ A. The write-protect hole is open.
- ☐ B. The write-protect hole is closed.
- ☐ C. The write-protect tab is placed over the write-protect hole.
- ☐ D. The DOS command WRITEPRO is used.

The correct answer is **A.** To write protect data on a microfloppy disk, the hole must be open. Refer to the "Floppy Disk Drive Construction" section for more information.

4. What is the maximum number of devices the secondary channel of the EIDE interface can support?

- ☐ A. One
- ☐ B. Two
- ☐ C. Three
- ☐ D. Four

The answer is **B.** Two devices can be attached to the secondary channel and two can be attached to the primary channel. Refer to the "EIDE Interface Standard" section for more information.

5. What is the maximum data transfer rate of the Wide Ultra 2 SCSI-3 bus?

- ☐ A. 40MB/sec
- ☐ B. 80MB/sec
- ☐ C. 20MB/sec
- ☐ D. 33MB/sec

The correct answer is **B.** The maximum speed of the Wide Ultra 2 SCSI-3 bus is 80MB/sec. Refer to the "SCSI Interface Standard" section for more information.

6. **Fast Wide or Wide Ultra SCSI-3 interface buses use which connector?**

    ☐ A. 36-pin
    ☐ B. 50-pin
    ☐ C. 60-pin
    ☐ D. 68-pin

The correct answer is **D.** Fast Wide or Wide Ultra SCSI-3 buses use a 68-pin connector and a 68-conductor cable. Refer to the "SCSI Interface Standard" section for more information.

7. **How can two HDDs be configured for installation on one EIDE channel?**

    ☐ A. By setting jumpers on the primary and secondary channels
    ☐ B. By setting jumpers on the EIDE HDDs for a master and slave configuration
    ☐ C. By using a separate cable attached to the primary and secondary channel connectors
    ☐ D. By using the DOS program CONFIG.SYS

The correct answer is **B.** For two EIDE devices to function on the same channel, they must be configured in a master/slave arrangement. Refer to the "EIDE Interface Standard" section for more information.

8. **How many conductors are there in a HDD and a FDD flat ribbon cable, respectively?**

    ☐ A. 40 and 32
    ☐ B. 40 and 34
    ☐ C. 50 and 40
    ☐ D. 36 and 30

The correct answer is **B.** HDD flat ribbon cables contain 40 conductors and FDD cables include 34 conductors. Refer to the sections "EIDE Interface Standard" and "Replacing Floppy Disk Drives" for additional information.

9. What is considered a low-level format of hard and floppy disks?

☐ A. Physical formatting
☐ B. Logical formatting
☐ C. Installing partitions
☐ D. Installing the file system

The correct answer is **A.** Physical formatting is a low-level format process that is usually performed by the manufacturer. Refer to the "Formatting Disks" section for more information.

10. FAT32 is which of the following?

☐ A. A 32-bit disk file system
☐ B. A 32-bit disk partitioning system
☐ C. A 32-bit disk file sector
☐ D. A 32-bit disk cylinder

The correct answer is **A.** FAT32 is a 32-bit file system that is installed during HDD logical formatting. Refer to the "Formatting Disks" section for more information.

PC and Device Configuration

THIS CHAPTER EXPLAINS how a PC is configured so that the system software and hardware devices communicate and function together. It prepares you for A+ Core exam questions on the configuration and installation of expansion boards and adapter cards, and questions on how to resolve device conflicts. Upon completing this chapter, you also will be able to answer questions regarding system Interrupt-Request (IRQ) settings, input/output (I/O) addresses, and direct memory access (DMA) channel assignments.

Exam Material in This Chapter

Based on the Official Objectives

- Identify default IRQ settings, I/O addresses, and DMA assignments
- Know how to configure and install expansion boards and adapter cards

Based on the Author's Experience

- Expect questions on expansion bus slots and boards
- Anticipate questions on default IRQ setting assignments
- Learn the DMA channel default assignments
- Know selected I/O addresses
- Know how to configure expansion boards and adapter cards
- Be able to identify the types of expansion boards and adapter cards
- Anticipate questions regarding device conflict resolution
- Be able to identify system Plug-and-Play requirements
- Know how to set dual in-line package (DIP) switches and jumpers

Are You Prepared?

Test your knowledge with the following questions. Then you'll know if you're prepared for the material in this chapter or if you should review problem areas.

1. How many IRQ setting assignments can AT-class computers process?

☐ A. 8
☐ B. 11
☐ C. 16
☐ D. 20

2. Which DMA channel can be used for a 16-bit Small Computer System Interface (SCSI) host adapter card?

☐ A. 2
☐ B. 6
☐ C. 4
☐ D. 10

3. Serial port COM1 uses which of the following resource assignments?

☐ A. 03F8 to 03FF and IRQ4
☐ B. 02F8 to 02FF and IRQ5
☐ C. 03E8 to 03EE and IRQ4
☐ D. 02E8 to 02EE and IRQ6

Answers:

1. C   *AT-class computers can process 16 IRQ setting assignments. See the "Understanding PC Communication Pathways" section.*

2. B   *DMA channel 6 is available for 16-bit devices. See the "Understanding PC Communication Pathways" section.*

3. A   *I/O base addresses 03F8 to 03FF and IRQ4 are dedicated to serial port COM1. See the "Understanding PC Communication Pathways" section.*

Understanding PC Communication Pathways

Every hardware device and I/O port in the PC system communicates with the central processing unit (CPU) over one or more pathways or physical circuit traces. When several devices attempt to use the same pathway, a conflict occurs and the CPU may not be able to communicate with either device. Additionally, because most pathway assignments are reserved during the PC manufacturing process, only a few pathways are available for installing add-on or after-market hardware devices.

The communication pathways in the PC are the IRQ lines, I/O addresses, and DMA channels. They are often called the PC's system resources and are used not only for communication, but also to interface and control all system hardware devices and both serial and parallel I/O ports. Basically, the hardware devices and I/O ports must share and coexist with limited PC system resources.

PC System Resource Conflicts

For the A+ Core exam, you should know that conflicts occur when two or more devices are contending for the same system resource, such as IRQ lines, I/O addresses, and DMA channels. Also memorize the system device assignments for each system resource. At least five questions address this important topic.

Interrupt-Request Lines

When a hardware device or I/O port requires service or attention from the CPU, it transmits a signal over its assigned IRQ line. The interrupt controller, which exclusively manages interrupt signals for the CPU, intercepts the signal and notifies the CPU that an interrupt request has been made. The CPU places its current task on hold and executes an interrupt request routine based on the requesting device's IRQ priority. It then executes the appropriate routine or instruction on a priority basis.

Today's AT-class computers have 16 IRQ lines built into their system boards or motherboards. The IRQ default setting assignments are identified from 0 to 15 with the lower numbers receiving higher priority service. Table 8-1 summarizes the most common IRQ default setting assignments.

Table 8-1 Common IRQ Default Setting Assignments

IRQ Default Line Assignment	Device
NMI	Non-masked interrupt (reports parity errors)
0	System timer
1	Keyboard
2	Programmable interrupt controller
3	COM2 and/or COM4
4	COM1 and/or COM3
5	LPT2 or sound card
6	Floppy disk drive
7	LPT1
8	Real-time clock
9	Available, but should not be used if IRQ2 is in use
10	Available
11	Available
12	Available (PS/2 mouse)
13	Math coprocessor
14	Hard disk drive controller
15	Available

Figure 8-1 shows the Windows 95 system IRQ settings in the View Resources page tab on the Computer Properties sheet.

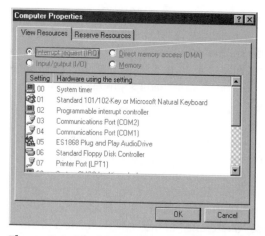

Figure 8-1 *The View Resources page tab on the Computer Properties sheet shows the Windows 95 system IRQ settings*

IRQ settings are made using either jumpers or DIP switches on the device's adapter card or the IRQ settings on the Resources page tab on the device's Properties sheet, as shown in Figure 8-2.

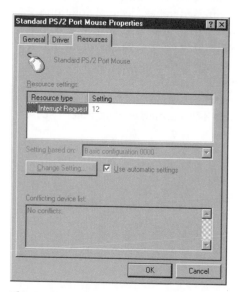

Figure 8-2 *The Resources page tab on the Standard PS/2 Port Mouse Properties sheet shows Interrupt Setting 12 and No conflicts*

It's extremely important that you memorize the default IRQ settings in Table 8-1, especially IRQ3, IRQ4, IRQ5, and IRQ7. Notice that these are the default settings for the serial and parallel I/O ports. Also, you should know that the IRQs with the lowest numbers receive the highest priority from the CPU.

There may be a question on the A+ Core exam on the total number of IRQ default setting assignments an Advanced Technology-class (AT-class) computer can process. The correct answer is 16 *if* the question does not refer to the non-masked Interrupt (NMI) assignment. However, if the question includes a reference to the NMI, the correct answer is 17 IRQ default setting assignments.

Input/output (I/O) addresses are main memory locations or segments specifically assigned to each hardware device and I/O port for communication and information exchange between itself and all other devices and ports in the PC system. Each device and port has a unique range of I/O addresses, which is expressed in hexadecimal notation.

I/O addresses can be compared to individual mailboxes at the post office. When the CPU or other hardware device wants to communicate with another device, it sends a message to the receiving device's mailbox or memory location. When the receiving device is ready to communicate with the sending device, it picks up the message and replies in the same mailbox or memory segment. Table 8-2 summarizes common I/O base address assignments.

Table 8-2 Common I/O Address Assignments

Common I/O Base Addresses	Devices
COM1	03F8 to 03FF
COM2	02F8 to 02FF
COM3	03E8 to 03EE
COM4	02E8 to 02EE
LPT1	0378 to 037F
LPT2	0278 to 027F
XT controller	0320 to 032F
Floppy disk controller	03F0 to 03F7
VGA	03C0 to 03CF

I/O address settings are made using either jumpers or DIP switches on the device's adapter card or the I/O address settings on the Resources page tab on the device's Properties sheet.

Figure 8-3 shows the Windows 95 system I/O address settings in the View Resources page tab on the Computer Properties sheet.

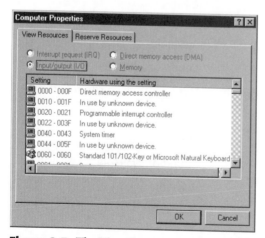

Figure 8-3 *The View Resources page tab on the Computer Properties sheet shows the Windows 95 system I/O address settings*

I/O Address Assignments

For the A+ Core exam, you should know that all hardware devices and I/O ports require a unique range of I/O addresses. You should also know the I/O address assignments for the serial and parallel I/O ports: COM1, COM2, COM3, COM4, LPT1, and LPT2.

Direct Memory Access Channels

Direct memory access (DMA) provides a direct, high-speed link between DMA hardware devices, such as Ultra DMA/33 hard disk drives, Ultra Wide SCSI host adapter cards, and main memory, bypassing the CPU. DMA also is useful when large blocks of data must be rapidly transferred to main memory. Without DMA, devices must access memory through the CPU. DMA speeds up the device's performance because it does not wait for the CPU to finish its current task.

Table 8-3 summarizes the DMA channel default assignments for AT-class computers.

Table 8-3 DMA Channel Default Assignments

DMA Channel Default Assignment	Device
0	Available
1	Sound or available
2	Floppy disk drive controller
3	Available
4	DMA cascade
5	Sound or available
6	Available
7	Available

DMA channel assignments 5-7 are used for 16-bit and 32-bit expansion boards and adapter cards, whereas assignments 0-3 are used for 8-bit boards and cards.

DMA channel assignments are made using either jumpers or DIP switches on the device's adapter card or the DMA settings or the Resources page tab on the device's Properties sheet.

You can view the Windows 95 system DMA settings using the View Resources page tab on the Computer Properties sheet, as shown in Figure 8-4.

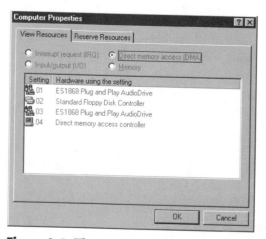

Figure 8-4 *The View Resources page tab on the Computer Properties sheet shows the Windows 95 system DMA settings*

Select the A+ Core exam answer choice that states DMA 6 can be used for a 16-bit adapter card.

Understanding Expansion Boards and Adapter Cards

Expansion boards and adapter cards are printed circuit boards (PCB) installed in the expansion bus slots on the system board or motherboard. Expansion boards add extra functionality to the computer, such as added memory, serial and parallel ports, disk drive controllers, and internal modems. Adapter cards are generally less complex than expansion boards because they simply enable the computer to use peripheral hardware devices, such as joysticks, CD-ROM drives, or SCSI devices.

Expansion board and adapter card design and construction are similar to that of the other circuit boards in the computer system. Expansion boards and adapter cards contain integrated circuits (also called *chips*), resistors, capacitors, diodes, connectors, sockets, and edge connectors mounted on a multi-layered core of non-conductive epoxy and fiberglass composite. The discrete components and parts are electrically connected by tiny copper foil traces (or *imprints*), forming circuits that perform specific electronic and logic functions. Expansion boards and adapter cards also contain either jumpers or DIP switches that enable the assignment of IRQ lines, I/O addresses, and DMA channels.

Figure 8-5 illustrates typical Peripheral-Component Interconnect (PCI) and Extended Industry Standard Architecture (EISA) expansion boards next to an Advanced Technology X (ATX) system board.

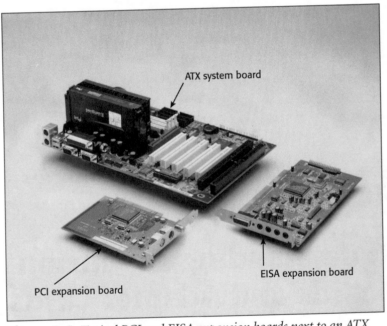

Figure 8-5 *Typical PCI and EISA expansion boards next to an ATX system board*

Although they are also used for many other purposes and functions, today's PCs include such adapter cards and expansion boards as video adapter cards, internal modems, sound cards, and Network Interface Cards (NIC).

Video Adapter Cards

Video adapter cards are circuit boards that translate output instructions from the CPU into data that can be displayed on the monitor screen. They are installed in expansion slots located on the system board, and the video signals are transmitted through a cable between the system unit case's back panel and the monitor. Video adapter cards usually contain on-board video RAM (VRAM) to speed up the complex calculations that render graphics and perform other graphics functions.

Modems

Modems (MOdulator/DEModulator) translate the computer's digital signals into analog signals for transmitting data over telephone lines, and they translate analog signals into digital signals for receiving data. Modems can be configured either as an internal circuit card installed in an expansion slot on the system board or as an external device connected to a serial port on the system unit case's back panel.

 An A+ Core exam question asks about the function of a modem. Select the answer choice stating that its function is to convert digital signals to analog and to convert analog signals to digital.

Sound Cards

Together with speakers and a microphone, sound cards enable sounds to be played back using various files and media, such as WAV, or Windows Sound Waveform files, Musical Instrument Data Interface (MIDI) files, and compact discs. Sound card designs use either frequency modulation (FM) synthesizers or wave table files that contain samples of instruments.

Network Interface Cards

Network Interface Cards (NICs) connect computers to local area networks (LANs). NICs are installed in expansion bus slots on the system board, and usually provide two types of connectors for the cables linking the computer with Ethernet LANs. RJ-45 connectors are used for connecting unshielded twisted-pair (UTP) cabling. Bayonet Naur Connector (BNC) connectors are used for connecting coaxial cabling.

Remember that UTP cables using RJ-45 connectors or coaxial cables using BNC connectors connect computers to Ethernet LANs.

Defining Expansion Bus Slots

Together with their associated expansion boards and adapter cards, the system board's expansion bus slots or expansion bus architectures define the amount of data that can be transferred at one time and the rates of data transfer. Newer Baby AT and ATX system boards often contain both 16-bit EISA and 32-bit PCI expansion slots, in addition to a single 32-bit AGP local-bus slot for an AGP video adapter card on the ATX boards. Older Full AT system boards often contain a combination of 8-bit ISA, 16-bit ISA, and 32-bit VESA slots. Figure 8-6 depicts EISA, PCI, and AGP expansion bus slots.

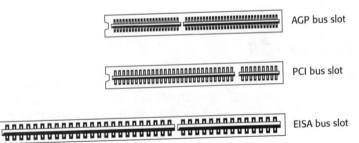

AGP bus slot

PCI bus slot

EISA bus slot

Figure 8-6 *EISA, PCI, and AGP expansion bus slots*

Industry-Standard Architecture Bus Slots

Originally introduced in the first IBM PC/XT in 1981, the 8-bit Industry-Standard Architecture (ISA) bus slot evolved into the 16-bit ISA bus slot with the introduction of the IBM PC/AT in 1984. The 16-bit ISA bus slot design is composed of two 8-bit ISA slots mounted end-to-end, permitting not only installation of 16-bit ISA expansion boards and adapter cards, but also the insertion of a single 8-bit ISA board or card. This feature is called *backward compatibility*.

Extended ISA Bus Slots

Developed by a group of computer companies in 1988 to update the ISA standards, EISA (Extended ISA) bus architecture has a 32-bit data path, and it is backward compatible with the older ISA standards. EISA operates at a much higher frequency and data transfer rate than ISA. Although they are found on many current system boards, the EISA bus slots are being phased out of the marketplace in favor of PCI bus slots exclusively.

Video Electronic Standards Association Local-Bus Slot

The 32-bit Video Electronic Standards Association (VESA) local-bus was developed in 1992 to communicate with the CPU at the CPU's speed. The VESA standard allowed for up to three slots to be built into a system board. It also facilitated bus mastering, which enabled *intelligent* VESA-compliant adapter cards to perform tasks independently of the CPU.

A version of the VESA local-bus called the VL-bus was developed specifically to accelerate video display signals. The new PCI local-bus architecture replaces the outdated VESA local bus and VL bus technologies.

Peripheral-Component Interconnect Local-Bus Slot

The 33MHz Peripheral-Component Interconnect (PCI) local-bus architecture, the new design standard for most Pentium-type system board expansion slots, supports either 32-bit or 64-bit bus slots. The PCI standard allows up to ten PCI expansion boards or adapter cards per system.

The PCI local-bus is self-configuring for Plug-and-Play (PnP) functionality, helping Windows 95, 98, and 2000 automatically detect and configure PnP expansion cards when they are installed in PCI slots. For PnP to function, the basic input/output system (BIOS) also must be PnP. PCI bus architecture also supports bus mastering.

 Watch for the A+ Core exam questions that ask about valid expansion bus slots located on PC system boards, such as ISA, EISA, VESA, and PCI. You will also be asked what the acronyms mean.

AGP Local-Bus (Video Only) Slot

Introduced by Intel with the Pentium II processor and 440LS and 440BX chip sets in 1997, the 66MHz AGP local-bus slot provides a direct path (also called *pipeline access*) from the CPU to the graphics accelerator rather than going through the 33MHz PCI local-bus. AGP slots dramatically increase video and graphics performance, and they are located on all ATX system boards. Future AGP bus slot designs will further increase clock speeds with corresponding increases in video and graphics performance.

True or False?

1. PCI local-bus architecture is either 16-bit or 32-bit wide at 66MHz speed.

2. COM3 uses I/O base address assignments 03C0 to 03CF.

3. DMA channel 6 can be used for a 16-bit expansion board and adapter card.

Answers: *1. False   2. False   3. True*

Installing and Configuring Expansion Boards and Adapter Cards

Although manufacturers often configure their hardware devices' expansion boards and adapter cards prior to shipment, it does not guarantee that the devices will work properly after installing them in the system. Several tasks including configuration, installation, and, possibly, conflict resolution, may have to be performed before a device installation is successful.

Configuration

Configuration means establishing communication between the device's expansion board or adapter card and the rest of the PC system by setting the device's IRQ, I/O address, and DMA assignments, as applicable. There are several alternative methods to accomplish this task:

- Permit the Windows 95 PnP feature to automatically configure the circuit board during boot up.

- Use the jumpers or the DIP switches on the circuit board to manually assign system resources to the device, as shown in Figure 8-7.

- Use the Windows 95 Device Manager (see Figure 8-8) to manually assign system resources to the device.

A successful configuration may involve a combination of two or all three methods.

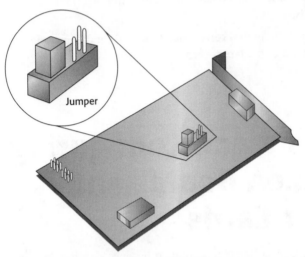

Figure 8-7 *The configuration jumpers on an expansion board*

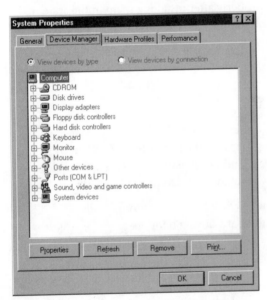

Figure 8-8 *Windows 95 Device Manager*

For PnP to function, the device, operating system, and system BIOS must be PnP-compliant.

Installation

Installing the device's expansion board or adapter card may come before or after configuration and the task requires the following steps:

1. Select the device's associated expansion bus slot on the system board. Note that the EISA expansion bus slot is brown or black and longer (see Figure 8-6) than the PCI bus slot, which is usually white.

2. Install the rear part of the circuit card's edge connector into the bus slot, and then firmly push down on the front top edge of the circuit card, securely seating the card in the slot.

3. Secure the circuit card slot plate to the system unit case using the single attachment screw.

4. Attach the interface cable(s).

5. Load the device driver.

Conflict Resolution

If the device, operating system, and system BIOS are PnP-compliant, the last step may not be necessary. The PnP device may function properly after boot up. However, if the device or another system device fails to function properly after boot up, chances are that a device conflict has occurred. In Windows 95, you can confirm this diagnosis by accessing the Device Manager (see Figure 8-8) and checking if a yellow exclamation mark, signifying a conflict, appears beside any device(s). The guidelines for conflict resolution are as follows:

1. Determine which devices cause the conflict.

2. Using Device Manager in Windows 95 or the Microsoft Diagnostics (MSD) utility program in MS-DOS, analyze the system resources to determine which resources are available to the offending devices.

3. Reconfigure the offending devices using either the jumpers or the DIP switches on the circuit card, or Device Manager to manually assign available system resources.

4. Reboot the computer.

 In Windows 95 Device Manager, a yellow exclamation mark beside a device means it has a system conflict.

Have You Mastered?

Now it's time to review the concepts in this chapter and apply your knowledge. These questions test your mastery of the material covered in this chapter.

1. AT-class computers use how many DMA channels?

- ☐ A. 7
- ☐ B. 8
- ☐ C. 5
- ☐ D. 6

The correct answer is **B.** AT-class computers use 8 DMA channels. Refer to the "Understanding PC Communication Pathways" section for more information.

2. Which component is not required for a device to be automatically configured?

- ☐ A. PnP CPU
- ☐ B. PnP operating system
- ☐ C. PnP device
- ☐ D. PnP BIOS

The correct answer is **A.** A CPU is not part of the PnP system. Refer to the "Installing and Configuring Expansion Boards and Adapter Cards" section for more information.

3. Which I/O ports are assigned IRQ4?

- [ ] A. COM1 and COM2
- [ ] B. COM2 and COM3
- [ ] C. COM1 and COM4
- [ ] D. COM1 and COM3

The correct answer is D. COM1 and COM3 are assigned IRQ4. Refer to the "Understanding PC Communication Pathways" section for more information.

4. Which I/O base address assignments are used for LPT1 and LPT2, respectively?

- [ ] A. 0271 and 0171
- [ ] B. 03E8 and 02E8
- [ ] C. 0378 and 0278
- [ ] D. 03F8 and 03E8

The correct answer is C. I/O addresses 0378 and 0278 are assigned LPT1 and LPT2, respectively. Refer to the "Understanding PC Communication Pathways" section for more information.

5. Which IRQ setting assignment cannot be used when installing an internal modem?

- [ ] A. IRQ11
- [ ] B. IRQ14
- [ ] C. IRQ 15
- [ ] D. IRQ10

The correct answer is B. IRQ14 cannot be assigned to any expansion board and adapter card because it is reserved for the hard disk drive controller. Refer to the "Understanding PC Communication Pathways" section for more information.

6. **Which IRQ address assignments are reserved for I/O ports LPT1 and LPT2, respectively?**

   ☐ A. IRQ7 and IRQ5
   ☐ B. IRQ6 and IRQ8
   ☐ C. IRQ3 and IRQ4
   ☐ D. IRQ1 and IRQ2

The correct answer is **A**. IRQ7 and IRQ5 are reserved for I/O ports LPT1 and LPT2, respectively. Refer to the "Understanding PC Communication Pathways" section for more information.

7. **Which IRQ address assignment is reserved for the floppy disk controller?**

   ☐ A. IRQ9
   ☐ B. IRQ6
   ☐ C. IRQ5
   ☐ D. IRQ7

The correct answer is **B**. IRQ6 is reserved for the floppy disk controller. Refer to the "Understanding PC Communication Pathways" section for more information.

8. **Which IRQ setting cannot be used if a video adapter card is already assigned to IRQ2?**

   ☐ A. IRQ3
   ☐ B. IRQ10
   ☐ C. IRQ9
   ☐ D. IRQ11

The correct answer is **C**. IRQ9 cannot be used if IRQ2 has already been assigned. Refer to the "Understanding PC Communication Pathways" section for more information.

9. How do you first configure a PnP NIC?

- ☐ A. Configure the NIC using the jumper assignment for the IRQ4 setting.
- ☐ B. Run the BIOS Setup program and change the NIC settings to IRQ6.
- ☐ C. Change CONFIG.SYS file using IRQ9.
- ☐ D. Start the computer and enable Windows 95 and PnP BIOS to configure the NIC.

The correct answer is **D**. To configure a PnP NIC, you can start the computer and enable Windows 95 and PnP BIOS to automatically configure the card. Refer to the "Installing and Configuring Expansion boards and Adapter Cards" section for more information.

10. Which COM ports use IRQ3?

- ☐ A. COM1 and COM2
- ☐ B. COM2 and COM4
- ☐ C. COM3 and COM4
- ☐ D. COM1 and COM4

The correct answer is **B**. COM2 and COM4 use IRQ3. Refer to the "Understanding PC Communication Pathways" section for more information.

Input and Output Peripheral Devices

THIS CHAPTER EXPLORES the computer's input and output peripheral hardware devices. It prepares you for A+ Core exam questions on keyboards, mice, video adapter cards, monitors, and modems. After completing this chapter, you also will be able describe the concepts, functions, design specifications, and servicing requirements of the input and output peripheral device.

Exam Material in This Chapter

Based on the Official Objectives

- Identify basic terms, concepts, and functions of peripheral devices
- Know how to install and configure peripheral devices
- Know how to service peripheral devices

Based on the Author's Experience

- Understand how keyboards, mice, monitors, and modems work
- Anticipate questions regarding modem speeds
- Be able to identify keyboard, mouse, monitor, video adapter card, and modem connectors
- Understand monitor features and specifications summarized in Table 9-1, "Video Display Standards"
- Learn the common modem control (AT) commands in Table 9-2
- Know how to fault-isolate and service input and output peripheral devices
- Expect questions regarding video card memory
- Memorize the modem hardware handshakes: Data Terminal Ready/Data Set Ready (DTR/DSR) and Request to Send/Clear to Send (RTS/CTS)

Are You Prepared?

Test your knowledge with the following questions. Then you'll know if you're prepared for the material in this chapter or if you should review problem areas.

1. What is the VESA video standard establishing a video design guideline of 800 × 600 pixel resolution and minimum 60Hz vertical refresh rate?

    ☐ A. VESA 600
    ☐ B. SVGA
    ☐ C. VGA
    ☐ D. EGA

2. What is dot pitch?

    ☐ A. The size of pixel diameters
    ☐ B. The angular difference between horizontal and vertical pixels
    ☐ C. The distance between pixels
    ☐ D. The size of phosphorous dots

3. When dialing a modem manually, what command followed by its number dials a touch-tone telephone?

    ☐ A. DDDL
    ☐ B. ATD
    ☐ C. DT
    ☐ D. ATDT

Answers:

1. B   *Super Video Graphics Array (SVGA) is the Video Electronics Standards Association (VESA) design standard establishing a video design guideline of 800 × 600 pixel resolution and 60Hz vertical refresh rate. See Table 9-1, "Video Display Standards."*

2. C   *Dot pitch is the distance between pixels measured in millimeters. See the "Understanding Monitors" section.*

3. D   *The AT modem command ATDT manually dials a touch-tone telephone. See the "Understanding Modems" section.*

Understanding Keyboards

The computer keyboard is an essential element to the computer's input, processing, storage, and output (IPSO) processing function. Originating from typewriter keyboards, modern computer keyboard designs use either a standard 101-key or a 104-key (also called Win95) layout. Portable computers use an 84-key layout.

A computer keyboard is made up of either capacitance or mechanical switches that convey information from the user to the computer. For example, depressing a key on the keyboard causes a change in the current flowing through the circuits associated with the depressed key. A built-in controller or microprocessor constantly scans these key circuits, and when it detects a keystroke, it generates a scan code that is sent to the Basic Input/Output System (BIOS). The BIOS then translates the scan code into ASCII, or machine language, that the computer understands. Figure 9-1 shows the built-in controller inside the keyboard.

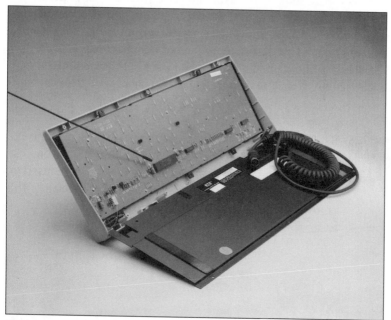

Figure 9-1 *A keyboard built-in controller*

Keyboard Connectors

The 104-key PS/2-style, or *enhanced,* keyboards use miniature DIN-6 style connectors. The 101-key IBM AT keyboards use DIN-5 connectors. The IBM AT connectors are slightly larger in diameter than the newer PS/2-style and contain one less pin.

Keyboard Servicing

Keyboard problems typically involve stuck keys and frayed connecting wires, but other problems, such as a lack of response to keystrokes or on-screen error messages indicating that the power-on self-test (POST) has not detected a keyboard, may occur. These problems can be easily isolated to the keyboard, system board, or device driver by exchanging the suspected faulty keyboard with a functioning one. Because keyboards are relatively inexpensive, replacing them is often better than repairing them.

The keyboard should not be disconnected while the computer is operating because severe damage can occur to the supporting circuitry on the system board. Additionally, the keyboard and mouse connections should not be reversed during computer boot or operation.

Rubbing alcohol, a mild detergent and water solution, a lint-free cloth, a vacuum cleaner, or compressed gas can all be used to clean keyboards.

Several A+ Core exam answer choices reference acetone as a preferred solvent to clean external surfaces of the computer. Acetone is highly corrosive and must never be used to clean plastic. Dismiss these answer choices immediately. The correct choice will probably reference mild detergent and water solution to clean external computer surfaces.

Understanding Mice

A mouse is a hand-held pointing device that controls the screen cursor and provides interaction between the user and the computer's operating system. It is an integral part of the graphical user interface (GUI) used by such GUI operating systems as Windows.

Mice use an optical-mechanical X-Y axis mechanism that controls the cursor by translating mechanical movement into directionally related electrical signals. Figure 9-2 illustrates the mouse's optical-mechanical X-Y mechanism. The mouse also provides an input signal to the GUI operating system when the user presses one of the mouse buttons. Mice are called *relative-pointing devices* because there are no defined limits to a mouse's movements and because the screen cursor does not directly track the mouse's movements.

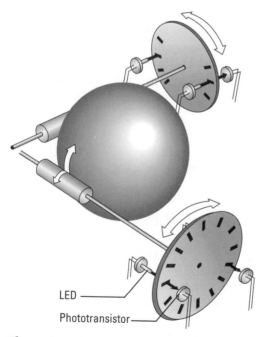

LED
Phototransistor

Figure 9-2 *A mouse's optical-mechanical axis mechanism*

Mouse Connectors

PS/2 mice use a 6-pin miniature DIN connector to connect to the ATX and Baby AT system boards. Other mice use a female DB9 connector or a female DB25 connector to connect to the serial port connectors on the computer's back panel.

Mouse Servicing

As with the keyboard, mice problems are obvious (for example, the mouse does not respond to user commands, or the mouse pointer, or cursor, does not appear on the screen). To isolate a mouse problem, exchange the suspected faulty mouse with a functioning mouse.

If the problem still exists, it may be because the mouse's device driver is not loaded into memory. A device driver is a small software routine that connects the peripheral hardware device to the operating system.

Additionally, the computer must always be shut down before replacing or installing a mouse because the mouse device driver is only loaded during boot.

Mice can be cleaned by first removing the ball and then cleaning the side rollers with a cotton swab dipped in alcohol. The ball can also be cleaned using rubbing alcohol.

Keyboards and Mice Connection Warning

You should know that the keyboard should remain connected while the computer is operating, and that the keyboard and mouse connections should not be reversed during computer boot or operation. Additionally, you should know that the mouse device driver must be loaded during computer boot before the mouse will work.

Understanding Monitors

Monitors play a central role in the computing process because they provide instant visual display and feedback to the user. Typical monitors are assemblies that usually include the video display, or cathode-ray tube (CRT), and the monitor housing, or cabinet. A video display adapter card (also called a *graphics card*), which is mounted in an expansion slot on the computer's system board, works in concert with the central processor unit (CPU) to provide the video signals to the monitor.

The CRT is designed around a vacuum tube that contains an electronic-gun assembly, an electromagnetic deflection yoke, and a curved or flat glass display screen. Figure 9-3 illustrates a CRT cross-section. The electronic gun shoots three beams across the inside front surface of the screen, which is coated with a phosphorous material that glows when irradiated. One beam elicits red light; one, green; and one, blue. The beams move across the screen left to right and top to bottom. They are deflected by the electromagnetic yoke, which receives signals from the CPU through the video card to set the scan rates, redraw time, and yoke direction. The beams refresh constantly to prevent the appearance of image flicker to the eye. The number of picture elements (pixels) on the screen determines the clarity of the image.

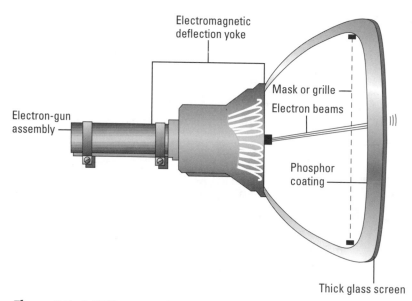

Figure 9-3 *A CRT cross-section*

Monitor Features and Specifications

Various design features and specifications define and categorize computer monitors:

- **Monitor size:** Monitor size is the diagonal measurement of the viewing area of the screen. Common sizes include 14, 15, 17, 19, and 21 inches.

- **CRT design type:** CRT design types include aperture grill, shadow mask, and slot mask.

- **Dot pitch:** Dot pitch is the distance between the pixels on the screen; the smaller the distance is, the crisper the image. Common dot pitches include .22, .25, .26, .27, and .28 millimeters.

- **Resolution:** Resolution is the number of pixels the monitor can display horizontally and vertically. Common resolutions include 640 × 480, 800 × 600, 1,024 × 768, 1280 × 1024, and 1600 × 1200.

- **Horizontal scan rate:** Horizontal scan rate is the number of times per second a line is redrawn horizontally or updated.

- **Refresh rate:** Refresh rate is the minimum number of times the entire screen can be updated or redrawn.

- **Color depth:** Video Graphics Array (VGA) monitors can display 16 colors at a resolution of 640 × 480 (4-bits). Super VGA (SVGA) and newer non-industry (VESA) standard monitors can display 16 colors, 256 colors (8-bits), 65,536 colors (16-bits), 16,777,216 colors (24-bits), and true color (30-bits).

 TEST TRAP You will be asked on the A+ Core exam about the definition of monitor dot pitch. Don't let the answer choices confuse you. Remember that dot pitch is the distance between pixels on the screen, and not the diameter of the pixel itself. Also the smaller the distance between pixels, the crisper the image is.

Servicing Monitors

After checking the contrast and brightness controls and the power switch, isolate a monitor that has no display or raster by exchanging it with a functional monitor. If the problem continues, exchange a potentially faulty video card with a functioning card.

In addition to not having a monitor display or raster, image degradation is sometimes a monitor problem (for example, image rolling, poor focus, flicker, snow, or black bands at the top and bottom of the screen may occur). Rather than opening the monitor housing to troubleshoot these problem symptoms yourself, have a qualified monitor repair technician service the monitor because monitors produce voltages that exceed 25,000 volts. Even after the computer is shut off, residual voltage can be stored in large capacitors or built up on the CRT's anode. Additionally, CRTs are vacuum-sealed and can implode if damaged.

POP QUIZ True or False?

1. The two types of switches used on most keyboards are capacitance and mechanical.

2. Monitors are constantly refreshed to prevent the appearance of image flicker to the eye.

3. No damage occurs if keyboards are exchanged while the computer is operating.

Answers: *1. True   2. True   3. False*

Understanding Video Adapter Cards

The video adapter card and monitor work in concert to generate maximum display resolutions and refresh rates. Video adapter cards include an accelerator chip, memory chips, and a digital-to-analog converter (DAC). The accelerator chip translates CPU instructions into lines, curves, and colors. Memory chips store the results, and the DAC converts the computer's digital data signals to analog signals that the monitor can process for a display.

Video Adapter Card Connectors

A female three-row 15-pin (DB15) connector is usually mounted on the slot plates of VGA and SVGA video adapter cards and connects to the monitor cable. Earlier video adapter cards used two-row connectors, older video adapter cards used only one DB15 connector and had no other connectors on the slot plate, and newer video adapter cards commonly include TV outputs.

Video Display Standards

Industry video display standards have been developed to standardize monitor and video card designs, as presented in Table 9-1. Note that the amount of simultaneous colors supported by a resolution is a function of not only the monitor, but depends on the memory installed on the video adapter card.

Table 9-1 Video Display Standards

Video Standards	Resolution (Horizontal × Vertical Pixels)	Supported Simultaneous Colors (Graphics Mode)	Minimum Vertical Refresh Rate (Hz)
CGA	320 × 200 640 × 200	4 2	60
EGA	640 × 350	16	60
VGA	640 × 480	16	60
SVGA	640 × 480 800 × 600 1024 × 768 1280 × 1024	256 16 and 256 16 and 256 16 and 256 (Depends on manufacturing)	60

Video Standards	Resolution (Horizontal × Vertical Pixels)	Supported Simultaneous Colors (Graphics Mode)	Minimum Vertical Refresh Rates (Hz)
XGA	1,024 × 768	256, 32K, or 16.7 million	44 (Interlaced)
Standard 1024	1,024 × 768	256, 32K, or 16.7 million	60
VESA 1280	1,280 × 1024	256, 32K, or 16.7 million	75

To prepare for the A+ Core exam, memorize all the monitor specifications and video display standards presented in Table 9-1.

Video Adapter Card Memory

Most memory used on video cards is dynamic random-access memory (DRAM), which is the same memory technology used to manufacture main memory or RAM. DRAM is the least expensive memory and is used on low- to mid-level performance video cards. Higher performance video card memory-types include video RAM (VRAM) and Windows RAM (WRAM).

One or two A+ Core exam questions ask about video memory. Select the answer choices that indicate VRAM and WRAM are higher quality but more expensive than regular DRAM.

Understanding Modems

Modems (a contraction of MOdulator/DEModulator) translate a computer's digital signals into analog signals for transmitting data over telephone lines. They also translate analog signals into digital signals for receiving data. Modems can be configured as either an internal circuit card installed in an expansion slot on the system board or an external device connected to a serial port on the system unit case's back panel.

Signal modulation and demodulation designs use the variances in amplitude of sound waves to transmit data over the telephone lines. The three common modulation designs are frequency-shift keying (FSK), phase-shift keying (PSK), and quadrature amplitude modulation (QAM).

Modem Speed

Modem performance is often categorized by baud rate. Baud rate is the number of events, or signal changes, that occur in one second. However, because one event can actually encode more than one data bit, a more accurate measure of today's high speed communications is the bit rate, or transfer rate, measured in bits per second (bps). For example, industry standards define modem designs in terms of bit rate, such as 28,800bps (the V.34), 33,600bps (the V.34bis), and 56,000bps (the V.90).

An additional factor that affects modem speed is the type of universal asynchronous receiver/transmitter (UART) chip installed in the computer's serial communication circuitry. The UART is a single integrated circuit (IC) that contains the receiving and transmitting circuits required for asynchronous serial communication. The three primary UART chip types are the 8250, 16450, and 16550. The 16550 UART is the latest and fastest UART chip, and it can replace older UART chips to increase serial communication speed.

Modem Commands

In most cases communication software programs automatically control modems. However, the control software can be manually superseded with the AT Command Set (Hayes codes), such as using the **ATDT12139736793** command to dial 1-213-973-6793 employing touch-tone dialing. All AT commands must be preceded with an **AT** prefix, which commands the modem's attention. Table 9-2 presents the most common modem or AT commands.

Table 9-2 Common Modem Control (AT) Commands

Command	Description
AT	Precedes all modem action commands
ATDT	Dials telephone numbers using touch-tone dialing
ATDP	Dials telephone numbers using pulse dialing
ATA	Answers an incoming call
ATH	Hangs up the modem
ATZ	Resets the modem to default

 Memorize the most common modem, or AT, commands in Table 9-2. You will definitely be asked about them on the A+ Core exam.

Serial Port Pin Assignments

An external modem communicates with its host computer using a modem cable attached to a serial port on the modem's back panel. The port connectors can be either a female 9-pin (DB9) or a female 25-pin (DB25) adhering to the RS-232C serial port design standard.

A hardware handshake is an exchange of signals over specific wires (other than the data wires), in which each device indicates its readiness to send or receive data. Table 9-3 summarizes the standard (RS-232C) serial port connector pin assignments for common hardware hand-shakes.

Table 9-3 Handshake Signals and Connector Pin Assignments

Handshake Signals	DB9 Pin Assignment	DB25 Pin Assignment
DTR (Data Terminal Ready)	4	20
DSR (Data Set Ready)	6	6
RTS (Request to Send)	7	4
CTS (Clear to Send)	8	5

For the A+ Core exam, memorize the following modem hardware handshakes: Data Terminal Ready/Data Set Ready (DTR/DSR) and Request to Send/Clear to Send (RTS/CTS). This knowledge will be worth one or two correct answers.

Two Registered Jack-11 (RJ-11) connectors also are located on the modem's back panel. They are usually configured in pairs, and labeled line and phone. The line jack connects the modem to a telephone wall jack using a standard telephone cable. The phone jack is used to connect a telephone to the modem.

When taking the A+ Core exam, don't confuse RJ-11 with RJ-45 connectors. RJ-11s are modem and standard telephone cable connectors, whereas RJ-45s are network cable connectors. RJ-11 connectors look like RJ-45 connectors, but they are smaller.

Have You Mastered?

Now it's time to review the concepts in this chapter and apply your knowledge. These questions test your mastery of the material covered in this chapter.

1. What type of memory is generally installed on low-performance video cards?

- ☐ A. XRAM
- ☐ B. WRAM
- ☐ C. VRAM
- ☐ D. DRAM

The correct answer is **D**. DRAM is generally installed on low-performance video cards. Refer to the "Understanding Video Adapter Cards" section for more information.

2. An external modem is usually connected to which port on the back panel of the computer's system unit case?

- ☐ A. RS-232C serial
- ☐ B. IEEE-1284 parallel
- ☐ C. LPT1
- ☐ D. SPP

The correct answer is **A**. An external modem is usually connected to the RS-232C serial port. Refer to the "Understanding Modems" section for more information.

3. A VGA monitor has what resolution?

☐ A. 640 × 350
☐ B. 1024 × 768
☐ C. 640 × 480
☐ D. 800 × 600

The correct answer is C. A VGA monitor has a resolution of 640 × 480. Refer to the "Monitor Features and Specifications" section for more information.

4. Which connector type is used on a modem to connect to a telephone line?

☐ A. RJ-11
☐ B. RJ-45
☐ C. BNC
☐ D. DB9

The correct answer is A. RJ-11 connectors are used to connect modems to telephone lines. Refer to the "Understanding Modems" section for more information.

5. Which connector is used on the modem's back panel to connect to the host computer?

☐ A. Male DB9
☐ B. Female DB25
☐ C. Male DB15
☐ D. RJ-45

The correct answer is B. A female DB25 or DB9 connector on the modem's back panel is usually used to connect to the host computer. Refer to the "Understanding Modems" section for more information.

6. Which AT command directs the modem to hang up?

- ☐ A. ATZ
- ☐ B. ATH
- ☐ C. ATX
- ☐ D. ATD

The correct answer is B. AT command ATH directs the modem to hang up. Refer to the "Understanding Modems" section for more information.

7. Which is the fastest UART chip?

- ☐ A. 16550
- ☐ B. 16555
- ☐ C. 17550
- ☐ D. 16540

The correct answer is A. The 16550 is the fastest UART chip. Refer to the "Understanding Modems" section for more information.

8. Which of the following will significantly improve image quality?

- ☐ A. Reducing the dot pitch
- ☐ B. Increasing the horizontal scan rate
- ☐ C. Increasing the display size by reducing the resolution
- ☐ D. Increasing the vertical refresh rate

The correct answer is A. Reducing the dot pitch will significantly improve the clarity and quality of the display image. Refer to the "Monitor Features and Specifications" section for more information.

9. Which of the following reduces the appearance of flicker to the eye?

- ☐ A. High refresh rate
- ☐ B. Low dot pitch
- ☐ C. High resolution
- ☐ D. Large display screen

The correct answer is A. A high refresh rate reduces the appearance of flicker to the eye. Refer to the "Understanding Monitors" section for more information.

10. **Which of the following acronyms is not a common communication handshake?**

☐ A. DTR
☐ B. DSR
☐ C. RTS
☐ D. HTS

The correct answer is D. HTS is not a common communication handshake. Refer to the "Understanding Modems" section for more information.

Printers

THIS CHAPTER ADDRESSES laser, inkjet, and dot matrix printers. It prepares you for A+ Core exam questions on how printers work. After completing this chapter, you also will be able to describe the various printer technologies, identify the primary printer components, and perform simple printer troubleshooting and preventive maintenance.

221

Exam Material in This Chapter

Based on the Official Objectives

- Identify basic printer concepts, operation, and components
- Identify common printer problems and service techniques

Based on the Author's Experience

- Understand the different printer technologies
- Anticipate questions on how printers work
- Be able to identify the primary printer components
- Expect questions that focus on laser printers
- Memorize the six steps in the printer image-formation process
- Know the causes of printer problems, including poor print quality
- Be able to identify printer connections and configurations
- Understand printer cleaning and preventive maintenance practices

Are You Prepared?

Test your knowledge with the following questions. Then you'll know if you're prepared for the material in this chapter or if you should review problem areas.

1. With a laser printer, why would several sheets pulled at once from the paper tray cause a paper jam?

□ A. The paper is too thick.
□ B. The paper is packed too tightly.
□ C. The paper has too much moisture.
□ D. The paper is too thin.

2. The sequence of events in the printer image-formation process is:

□ A. Fusing, conditioning, writing, transferring, charging, and cleaning
□ B. Conditioning, writing, transferring, charging, fusing, and cleaning
□ C. Cleaning, conditioning, transferring, writing, charging, and fusing
□ D. Cleaning, conditioning, writing, developing, transferring, and fusing

3. What causes a laser printer to print completely black pages ?

☐ A. The thermal switch in the fuser assembly is malfunctioning.
☐ B. The transfer corona wire is defective.
☐ C. The laser scanner assembly is defective.
☐ D. The primary corona wire is defective.

Answers:

1. B   *Paper that is packed too tightly can cause a paper jam by pulling several sheets at once from the paper tray. See Table 10-1," Laser Printer Problems and Causes."*

2. D   *The sequence of events in the printer image-formation process is cleaning, conditioning, writing, developing, transferring, and fusing. See the "How Laser Printers Work" section.*

3. D   *A defective primary corona wire can cause a laser printer to print completely black pages. See Table 10-1, "Laser Printer Problems and Causes."*

Printer Technology

Printers are categorized by their print technology, which defines how the image is produced on paper. The three types of print technology are laser, inkjet, and dot matrix.

Laser Printers

Similar to the technology used by copiers, laser printers employ the electrophotographic process (EP) that combines electricity, laser light, and powered ink to reproduce images. Basically, the process consists of painting an electrostatic image of an entire page on a photosensitive drum using a laser beam. When toner is applied to the drum, a powered ink image is created as the toner adheres only to the sensitized areas of the drum. The ink image is transferred to the paper page as the drum rotates and presses against the page and the transfer roller. The image is then permanently bonded to the page as it passes through the fusing roller mechanism. Figure 10-1 shows a laser printer with the toner cartridge removed. The advantages to laser printers include high print quality, low cost per printed page, and fast printing speeds.

Figure 10-1 *A laser printer with toner cartridge removed*

Inkjet Printers

Inkjet printers use a simple and low-cost printer technology. Thermal inkjet technology employs an electrical pulse, which heats a resistor that boils ink in the firing chamber of the print head, instantly forming a vapor bubble. Pressure created by the bubble pushes ink through a nozzle, forming a droplet that is deposited onto the paper. When the resistor cools, the vapor bubble collapses and suction pulls new ink from the reservoir into the firing chamber. Figure 10-2 shows an inkjet printer and its disposable print head and ink cartridge assembly.

Although inkjet printers produce good quality printouts, one disadvantage is that their print head nozzles can be easily clogged by dry ink if the print head is not parked at *home*. Home is the area at the end of the carriage assembly where the print head is parked while the printer is not in use. Clogged nozzles result in incomplete printed characters and images, or no printouts altogether. Another disadvantage to inkjet printers is that their ink cartridges can run out of ink without prior warning.

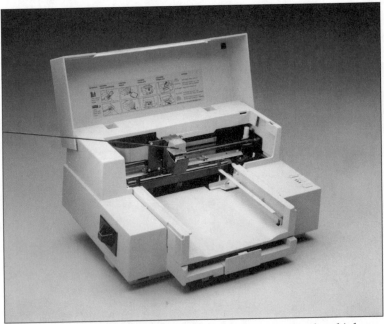

Figure 10-2 *An inkjet printer and its disposable print head and ink cartridge assembly*

Dot Matrix Printers

Dot matrix (also called *impact*) printers use a print head containing either 9 or 24 tiny pins that strike, or impact, an inked ribbon and paper, pressing dots of ink from the ribbon to the paper. A series of dots create characters that are defined by commands and data files of codes received from the computer. Figure 10-3 shows a dot matrix printer and its print head.

While dot matrix printers are relatively noisy, one advantage is that extreme temperatures, dust, and vibrations, such as those from alternative printer types, do not affect their print heads. Another advantage is that they can also print on multi-part and *tractor feed* paper.

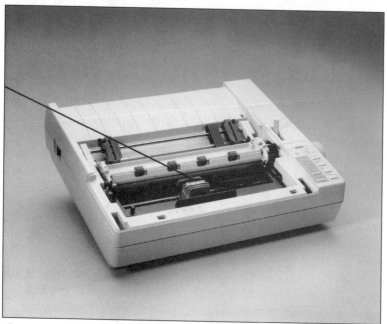

Figure 10-3 *A dot matrix printer and its print head*

Printer Advantages and Disadvantages

You should know the following advantages and disadvantages to the three printer technologies:

- Laser printers produce printed pages that are low cost and high quality at high speeds.

- Inkjet printers produce printed pages that are good quality, but their print head nozzles can be easily clogged with dry ink if they are not parked at *home*.

- Dot matrix printers are not affected by extreme temperatures, dust, and vibration. They can also print on multi-part and tractor feed paper.

How Laser Printers Work

EP laser printers employ an image-formation system (IFS) electro-mechanical design. The IFS design incorporates multiple components or assemblies in the printing process rather than the relatively simple print head and carriage assemblies used by inkjet and dot matrix printers. Many of the movable IFS mechanisms experience wear, which increases part tolerances and decreases reliability and print quality.

The replaceable toner cartridge is the key to maintaining high reliability and print quality because it contains many of the primary IFS components. When the toner is used up and the cartridge must be replaced, the primary components also are renewed.

The plastic toner cartridge contains the toner, which is a very fine dry powder composed of organic compounds (epoxy) bound to iron particles within the toner cylinder, the Electrophotographic (EP) drum, the cleaning blade, erase lamps, and the primary corona wire, as shown in Figure 10-4.

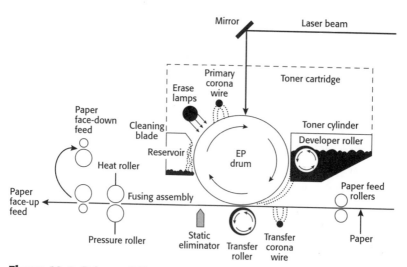

Figure 10-4 *Primary IFS components*

The primary IFS components in further detail are as follows:

- **Toner cylinder:** The toner cylinder contains the toner, the developer roller, and the cleaning blade, which is made of rubber and located along the length of the drum; it gently scrapes away residual toner from the EP drum, returning the excess toner to its reservoir.

- **EP drum:** The EP drum is at the heart of the printing process. It is made of aluminum and coated with a thin film of photosensitive zinc oxide that changes its electrical charge state when exposed to light. Never open the flap on a new toner cartridge or the EP drum will be exposed to ambient light, effectively destroying it.

- **Erase lamps:** The erase lamps are used to discharge the EP drum by shining a filtered light along the length of the drum.

- **Primary corona wire:** The primary corona is a thin wire located close to the EP drum. When a high negatively charged voltage ($-$ 6000 volts) is applied to the primary corona wire and the regulating voltage grid, a corona or electrical field is created around the wire that charges the drum from $-$ 600 volts to $-$ 1000 volts.

- **Laser:** The beam from a laser is used to *paint* images on the EP drum's surface. Note the three primary types of IFS writing mechanisms in order of efficiency are the laser light-emitting diodes (LEDs), and liquid crystal shutters (LCSs).

- **Transfer corona wire:** The transfer corona is a thin wire that positively charges the paper in order to transfer the toner image from the drum to the paper.

- **Transfer roller:** The transfer roller assists in transferring the toner image to the paper.

- **Static eliminator:** The static eliminator electrically neutralizes the paper.

- **Fusing assembly:** The fusing assembly consists of a heat roller and a pressure roller that melts and pressurizes the toner in order to permanently fuse or bond the image to the paper.

For the A+ Core exam, remember that the three primary types of IFS writing mechanisms in order of efficiency are (1) laser, (2) light-emitting diodes (LEDs), and (3) liquid crystal shutters (LCSs). Additionally, remember that the primary corona wire charges the EP drum with between – 600 volts to – 1000 volts.

Not only are toner cartridges easy to replace but they also provide a clean and simple method of toner replacement and primary IFS component renewal. Used toner cartridges should not be discarded because they are recyclable. However, if toner cartridges are discarded, special disposal procedures do not have to be followed.

On the A+ Core exam question regarding which component does not require special disposal procedures, select the toner cartridge. Batteries, CRTs, and cleaning solvents require special disposal procedures.

The EP Laser Printing Process

Following is a step-by-step description of the EP laser printing process:

1. **Drum cleaning:** To prepare the photosensitive drum for the laser printing process, a rubber blade applied along the length of the rotating drum gently scrapes away residual toner. Additionally, a series of erase lamps electrically removes the previous image from the drum, leaving it in a neutral electrical state. Specks or dots appear on the printed pages if the cleaning task is not performed adequately.

2. **Drum charging or conditioning:** To become light sensitive, the EP drum is charged to a range from – 600 volts to – 1000 volts. This task is performed by applying a high negative charging voltage (approximately −6000 volts) to the primary corona wire and the regulating voltage grid, creating a corona, or electrical field, around the primary corona wire assembly. The corona ionizes the air molecules surrounding the corona wire assembly, and uniform negative charges migrate to the surface of the EP drum.

3. **Electrical image writing:** To form the electrical image on the EP drum, the laser beam scans the drum's surface, discharging the precise areas of image formation. The laser beam causes a much weaker negatively charged image area on the drum, which corresponds to the image area on the paper after development.

4. **Electrical image developing:** To change the invisible electrical image represented by relatively weak negative charges into a visible or developed image, the developer roller transfers toner to the EP drum. Because the toner contains negatively charged iron particles, it is attracted to only the areas exposed to the laser beam and repelled by the other uniformly strong negatively charged areas of the drum.

5. **Toner image transferring:** The toner representing the image is then transferred to a paper sheet using the transfer corona wire, which charges the incoming paper page with a powerful positive charge. This positive charge strongly attracts the negatively charged toner particles, and they migrate from the EP drum to the page assisted by the transfer roller.

6. **Toner image fusing:** Because the toner is simply held on the page with a small electrostatic charge, the toner image is fused or permanently bonded to the paper by passing it between two fusing rollers. The top roller applies heat and works with the bottom roller to apply pressure to melt and press the toner image into the paper. A thermal fuse that acts as a thermostat protects the image fusing assembly from overheating.

Remember that a thermal fuse that acts as a thermostat protects the image fusing assembly from overheating. No other thermostats exist in a laser printer.

Six Steps in the Image Formation Process

For the A+ Core exam, you should know the following six steps in the image-formation process:

1. Cleaning
2. Charging
3. Writing
4. Developing
5. Transferring
6. Fusing

Also remember that cleaning is the first step in the process.

Servicing Printers

Because printers contain paper feed roller and gear mechanisms, and print head carriage assemblies, and they often operate in environments filled with dust, oil, and ink, performing preventive maintenance in accordance with the manufacturer's recommendations greatly lessens the chance of problems. But problems still may occur.

Recycling the power can often clear printer problems. Interface cabling or the host computer also can cause printer problems. For example, if a laser printer does not print but passes a self-test with a clean test page, check the connections on the interface cable between the host computer and printer for electrical and mechanical integrity. Then check the host computer for problems, such as an Incompatible printer driver error message. Lastly, perform fault diagnostics.

Don't fall for the A+ Core exam answer choices that reference complex printer fault diagnostics as the first step in solving the problem presented in the question. The correct answer is much easier: Simply recycle the power and check the integrity of the interface cable before performing more extensive troubleshooting.

The following sections provide general guidelines for troubleshooting and servicing printers.

Servicing Laser Printers

Laser printer problems often appear in either the quality of the printed pages or in error code messages. Table 10-1 provides examples of laser printer problem symptoms and possible causes.

Table 10-1 Laser Printer Problems and Causes

Problem Symptoms	Possible Causes
Totally black page	Defective primary corona wire
Totally white page	Defective transfer corona
No printing after self-test	Connections lost between the host computer and printer
Vertical fade or white streaks	Low toner supply or dirty debris-fouled transfer corona wire
Faded print characters	Dirty corona wire
Smearing	Dirty or defective fusing mechanism
Repetitive defects	Sticky or defective paper transport rollers
Paper curl	Defective fuser assembly
Badly formed characters	Paper stock too slick or defective laser scanner assembly
Several sheets pulled from tray at one time, causing paper jam	Paper packed too tightly, possesses static electricity, or incorrect weight
Error 20	Insufficient memory

True or False?

1. The first step in the laser printing process is charging the EP drum.
2. The regulating voltage grid reduces and regulates the voltage to the photosensitive drum in a laser printer.
3. The inkjet printer is part of the image-formation family of printers.

Answers: *1. False   2. True   3. False*

Servicing Inkjet Printers

As with laser and dot matrix printers, the first step when troubleshooting inkjet printer problems is to determine whether the printer, host computer, or interface cable is defective. If the printer is the problem, performing a self-test and following the manufacturer's maintenance manual instructions often reveals the exact cause of the problem. Table 10-2 provides examples of inkjet printer problem symptoms and possible causes.

Table 10-2 Inkjet Printer Problems and Causes

Problem Symptoms	Possible Causes
No power-on light or typical operating noise	Printer is *off-line*, power supply fuse blown, or power supply defective
Faint, uneven, or lack of printed characters	Low or empty ink supply in the ink cartridge or clogged print head nozzles
Print head printing but not moving	Defective timing belt, home positioning sensor, print head positioning motor, or control circuit board
Paper not advancing	Defective gear train or feed motor

Some inkjet printers, such as those manufactured by Hewlett-Packard and Epson, feature print heads built into each ink cartridge. Replacing the ink cartridge/print head modules on a regular basis helps keep the nozzles from clogging with foreign particles or dried ink, and maintains constant print quality and reliability.

Servicing Dot Matrix Printers

Because dot matrix printers contain many assemblies and moving parts, they have a number of components that are potential problems, such as the print head, ribbon feed motor, ribbon, line feed motor, and control circuit board. Table 10-3 presents examples of dot matrix printer problem symptoms and possible causes.

Table 10-3 Dot Matrix Printer Problems and Causes

Problem Symptoms	Problem Causes
No power-on light or typical noise	Printer is *off-line*, power supply fuse blown, or power supply defective
Faint, uneven, not fully-formed, or lack of printed characters	Worn, dried-up, or old ink ribbon; incorrect gap between platen and print head; defective print head or pins
Light, then dark printed characters	Defective ribbon drive stepper motor
Printing shuts down after operating satisfactorily	Defective print head thermostat (If the printer head slows down, the thermostat is doing its job)
Prints continuously on same line	Defective line space stepper motor
Print head printing but not moving	Defective timing belt, home positioning sensor, print head positioning motor, or control circuit board

Don't be fooled by an A+ Core exam question on why the dot matrix printer is slowing down after printing numerous pages. The correct answer is that the printer does not have a problem because the print head thermostat is doing its job; it provides feedback signal to the printer's controller, which then slows the printer down in order to extend the life of the print head.

Defining Printer Interfaces, Cables, and Connectors

To function, printers must communicate, or interface, with a host computer. The three common printer interfaces are RS-232C serial, Centronix parallel, and IEEE 488.

The RS-232C Serial Interface

Serial printers communicate one bit at a time with their host computer using the common COM1 or COM2 ports on the back panel of the computer. Serial data communication is fast and can transmit data over long distances. Serial printer interface cables usually have either male or female 9-pin D-subminiature (also called DB9) connectors at both ends.

The Centronix Parallel Interface

Centronix is the standard for data communication between parallel printers and the LPT1 (Line PrinTer1) or LPT2 ports on IBM PC-compatible host computers. It transfers eight bits (or one byte) simultaneously over eight separate wires in one direction. Because a Centronix-type connector is mounted on parallel printers, the Centronix parallel interface cable has a 36-pin Centronix connector on one end and a male or female 25-pin (also called DB25) on the other end.

TEST TIP One A+ Core exam question asks what kind of connector is mounted on a parallel printer. Select 36-pin Centronix.

The IEEE 488 Parallel Interface

Not as common as serial and Centronix interface standards, the Institute of Electrical and Electronic Engineers (IEEE) 488 (also called GPIB or *general-purpose interface bus*) parallel interface supports bi-directional and network communications. Hewlett-Packard printers and plotters use the GPIB.

Printer Interface Cables and Connectors

You should know the following key points regarding printer interface cables and connectors:

- Serial printers communicate one bit at a time using RS-232C interface cables that have 9-pin D-subminiature (also called DB9) connectors at both ends.

- Parallel (Centronix and IEEE-488) printers communicate eight bits or one byte of data at a time using an interface cable with a 36-pin Centronics connector at one end and a 25-pin connector at the other end.

Have You Mastered?

Now it's time to review the concepts in this chapter and apply your knowledge. These questions test your mastery of the material covered in this chapter.

1. In an inkjet printer, a partially clogged print head nozzle is likely to cause which of the following symptoms?

☐ A. Smeared ink across the entire page
☐ B. Incomplete print characters
☐ C. Paper jam
☐ D. Totally black page

The correct answer is **B**. A partially clogged print head nozzle is likely to cause an incomplete print character. Refer to Table 10-2, "Inkjet Printer Problems and Causes," for more information.

2. Which component in a laser printer should never be exposed to ambient light?

☐ A. The primary corona wire
☐ B. The transfer corona wire
☐ C. The laser scanner assembly
☐ D. The photosensitive drum

The correct answer is **D**. The photosensitive drum must never be exposed to ambient light. Refer to the "How Laser Printers Work" section for more information.

3. **In a laser printer, a thermal fuse is used to prevent which of the following?**

    ☐ A. The high-voltage power supply from overheating
    ☐ B. The laser beam power package from overheating
    ☐ C. The fusing assembly from overheating
    ☐ D. The electronic control package from overheating

The correct answer is C. The thermal fuse is used to prevent the fusing assembly from overheating. Refer to the "How Laser Printers Work" section for more information.

4. **What is the next task to perform if a non-networked laser printer still does not print after it has successfully passed self-test?**

    ☐ A. Check for a fusing assembly error or malfunction
    ☐ B. Check the printer interface cable for problems
    ☐ C. Check the paper pickup roller
    ☐ D. Check the laser scanning assembly

The correct answer is B. Check the host computer-to-printer cable for problems following a successful printer self-test. Refer to the "Servicing Laser Printers" section for more information.

5. **What is the surface charge on a photosensitive drum in a laser printer?**

    ☐ A. – 600 volts
    ☐ B. + 600 volts
    ☐ C. – 6000 volts
    ☐ D. + 6000 volts

The correct answer is A. The surface charge on the photosensitive drum is between – 600 and – 1000 volts. Refer to the "How Laser Printers Work" section for more information.

6. What causes the firing chamber nozzle in an inkjet printer's print head and ink cartridge to discharge an ink droplet?

☐ A. Pressure from the solenoid unit
☐ B. Pressure from a vapor bubble
☐ C. Pressure created by the power head assembly
☐ D. Positive charge on the paper attracts the negatively charged ink

The correct answer is **B**. Pressure from a vapor bubble causes the firing chamber nozzle in an inkjet printer to discharge an ink droplet. Refer to the "Printer Technology" section for more information.

7. What causes a laser printer to print blank, white sheets of paper?

☐ A. The transfer corona wire is defective
☐ B. The fusing assembly is malfunctioning
☐ C. The primary corona assembly is defective
☐ D. The erasure lamps are defective

The correct answer is **A**. A defective transfer corona causes a laser printer to print blank, white sheets of paper. Refer to Table 10-1, "Laser Printer Problems and Causes," for more information.

8. The printer to use for a multi-part form is which of the following?

☐ A. Laser
☐ B. Dot Matrix
☐ C. Inkjet
☐ D. Bubble Jet

The correct answer is **B**. A dot matrix (or other impact-printer types) is the only printer that can print a multi-part form. Refer to the "Printer Technology" section for more information.

9. **Which of the following components in a laser printer should you not expose to ambient light?**

   ☐ A. The ozone filter
   ☐ B. The fusing assembly
   ☐ C. The toner cartridge
   ☐ D. The EP drum

The correct answer is **D**. The EP drum should never be exposed to ambient light. Refer to the "How Laser Printers Work" section for more information.

10. **What occurs during the transfer stage in the laser printer process?**

   ☐ A. The electrical image is transferred to the photosensitive drum using the laser.
   ☐ B. The toner image is transferred from the photosensitive drum to the paper.
   ☐ C. The negative charge is transferred to the photosensitive drum using the primary transfer wire assembly.
   ☐ D. The fuser assembly transfers the image to the paper using heat and pressure.

The correct answer is **B**. The toner image is transferred from the photosensitive drum to the paper during the transfer stage in the laser printer process. Refer to the "How Laser Printers Work" section for more information.

Networking Basics

THIS CHAPTER PRESENTS the basics of computer networks. It prepares you to correctly answer A+ Core exam questions on local area networks (LANs), metropolitan area networks (MANs), and wide area networks (WANs). After completing this chapter, you also will be able to answer questions on network topologies, architectures, protocols, hardware, and software. Additionally, you will be able to define the important network Open System Interconnection (OSI) Model.

Exam Material in This Chapter

Based on the Official Objectives

- Identify basic network terms, concepts, and functions
- Know how to service networked computers and peripheral devices

Based on the Author's Experience

- Understand network configurations: LANs, WANs, and MANs
- Expect questions on LANs: Client/server and peer-to-peer
- Anticipate questions on network topologies: Star, bus, and star-wired token ring
- Know about network Media Access Control (MAC) types, such as Ethernet and token ring
- Anticipate questions about the network OSI Model and protocols
- Be able to identify network cables and connectors
- Expect questions addressing networking peripherals, such as Network Interface Cards (NICs), hubs, bridges, switches, routers, and gateways

Are You Prepared?

Test your knowledge with the following questions. Then you'll know if you're prepared for the material in this chapter or if you should review problem areas.

1. Novell client/server networks use which type of primary protocol?

☐ A. NetBEUI
☐ B. NetBIOS
☐ C. IPX/SPX
☐ D. NOVELL.25

2. The maximum segment length of 10base-T cable is which of the following?

☐ A. 500 meters
☐ B. 100 meters
☐ C. 200 meters
☐ D. 2000 meters

3. Ethernet uses which type of network access method?

☐ A. CSMA/CD
☐ B. Token Ring
☐ C. ARCnet
☐ D. Full duplex

Answers:

1. C   *Novell networks primarily use the Internet Packet eXchange/ Sequenced Packet eXchange (IPX/SPX) protocol. See the "Understanding Network Protocols" section.*

2. B   *The maximum length of a 10base-T cable segment is 100 meters. See Table 11-1, "Ethernet Cable Specifications."*

3. A   *Ethernet uses the Carrier Sense Multiple Access/Collision Detection (CSMA/CD) network access method. Refer to the "Defining Ethernet Architecture" section.*

Understanding Computer Networks

A computer network is a collection of interconnected computing devices that enable a community of people to share information and resources, such as file, printing, message (electronic mail with attachments), hard-disk space, communication, and terminal emulation (remote access) services. Networks can range from several computers in an office sharing a printer to thousands of computers in many countries around the world exchanging information. The three types of network configurations are LANs, WANs, and MANs.

Local Area Networks

A local area network (LAN) is a group of computers that occupies a relatively small geographical area, such as a school computer lab, office, or building. In a LAN, the computers are typically interconnected and share services using NICs, network cabling, network operating systems (NOSs), and networking peripherals.

The two principal types of LANs are client/server (also called *server-based*) and peer-to-peer. The server-based network relies on one or more servers that are dedicated to providing all the services required by dozens or even hundreds of client computers on the network. In peer-to-peer networking, the server functions are distributed among several computers on the LAN.

Client/server LANs

With client/server LANs, a large and powerful server is at the heart of a relatively small, single-server network (also called *centralized network*). It provides the file, print, hard-disk space, and communication services required by all its client computers. In larger server-based networks, multiple servers provide the various computing services to the entire LAN. In multiple-server networks (also called *distributed networks*), the servers' duties can be distributed in a way that maximizes network performance. For example, the client computers can be split into workgroups, and each group can be assigned a specific server. Similarly, the server's duties can be distributed among the servers, such as assigning the responsibilities for the file services to one server and the print services to another.

The server computer is usually equipped with multiple hard disk drives, backup tape or external hard disk drives, and CD-ROM Array drives. In addition to the file, print, disk-space, and communication services, the server-based operating system runs a variety of powerful LAN management and auditing programs.

Each client computer runs its own application programs, and its networking software redirects requests for file and print to the network server and network operating system.

The client/server type of network is robust and provides excellent user-level security compared to peer-to-peer networks. This type of network must use a NOS such as Microsoft's Windows NT, Windows 2000, or Novell's NetWare. A server/client network has a high installation cost, but the cost-per-client computer declines as more peer computers are added to the network. A client/server network is ideal for LANs with ten or more computers.

Peer-to-peer LANs

In peer-to-peer networks (also called *collaborative networks*), no single computer provides all the networking services. Instead, all the computers have equal status and each computer can act as both a server and a client in the network.

When acting as a server, each computer can share any of its resources with the network, and it can also control (password-protected) access to its shared resources. On the client side, each computer in the network that has permission can access any of the other peer computers' resources.

In general, peer-to-peer networks offer low start-up costs, simplicity, and sufficient power for LANs that contain ten or fewer computers. Additionally, Windows for Workgroups 3.11, Windows 95, and Windows 98 are designed to support peer-to-peer networks.

Client/server LANs are more robust and have better user-level security than peer-to-peer LANs.

Metropolitan Area Networks

A metropolitan area network (MAN) is a group of LANs spread over a geographical area the size of a campus, industrial park, or city. LANs are generally linked with leased digital telephone lines, Fiber Distributed Data Interface (FDDI) lines, DQDB Distributed Queue Dual Bus (DQDB) lines, or digital microwave sites.

Wide Area Networks

Wide area networks (WANs) interconnect two or more LANs, or other WANs across cities, states, countries, and even the world. The networks within a WAN are usually connected using various high-speed, long-distance telecommunications, such as satellite links, circuit-switched digital services, and packet-switching services.

An enterprise network is a type of WAN that connects all the computers within an organization, regardless of their geographic location or networked protocols.

KNOW THIS Characteristics of Network Configurations

For the A+ Core exam, you should know the following network characteristics:

- LANs are geographically small — about the size of an office or building. They can be configured as either client/server or peer-to-peer.

- MANs are composed of interconnected LANs or groups of LANs, and they span about the size of a campus or city.

- WANs, consisting of interconnected LANs and MANs, are the largest network type and can cover a state, nation, or even the world, like the Internet does.

Understanding Network Topologies

The term topology is used to describe the physical layout of networks. It describes not only how the computers, servers, printers, and other peripherals are interconnected, but also how they connect to the specialized networking devices, such as hubs, switches, bridges, and routers. The three common network topologies are the star, bus, and star-wired token ring.

Star Network Topology

In a star network topology, each computer, server, and peripheral (each device is also called a *network node*) has a dedicated twisted-pair wire cable connecting it to a central network hub or concentrator. The hub generally amplifies the incoming signals and repeats or passes them on to the other network nodes so that each computer gains access to the other computers and devices on the network. Figure 11-1 depicts the star network topology.

The star network topology is ideal for peer-to-peer networks because all the computers and servers are physically connected in an equal status. It also has several reliability and servicing features. For example, the failure of one node will not affect the others in the network. Fault-isolation and statistical data collection tasks also are easier because the network signals pass through a single point or hub. However, the star-configured network does require a lot of cabling, which adds time and cost to its installation.

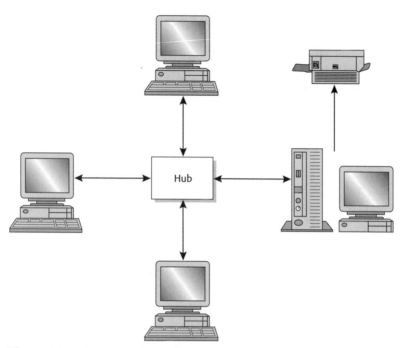

Figure 11-1 *Star network topology*

Star networks are the most popular LAN topology. Star network designs also are more reliable and maintainable than bus networks.

Bus Network Topology

In a large bus network topology, each computer, server, and peripheral device is attached to a single, common cable (called a *bus* or *backbone*) using a shorter cable (called a *drop-cable*), as depicted in Figure 11-2. The bus network topology is often used for networking an entire building when the backbone is hidden behind walls and the drop-cable connections can be easily made at wall jacks.

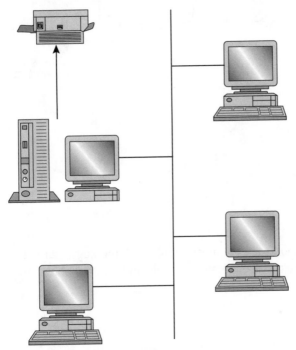

Figure 11-2 *Bus network topology*

In small bus networks, individual coaxial cables, BNC connectors, T-connectors, and terminators can be used to interconnect the computers and devices in a serial arrangement that does not require a single, common cable for a backbone. Although small bus networks have low setup costs, a major disadvantage to this network configuration is that failure of a single node connection causes the entire network to fail.

Additionally, one end of the small bus (and large bus) network must be grounded and the other end terminated.

Star-wired Token Ring Network Topology

Star-wired token ring network topology enhances and essentially replaces the older token ring topology. Networks based on star-wired token ring topology have nodes emanating from a special kind of hub called a Multistation Access Unit (MAU). Unlike the standard star network hub in which data packets are assigned specific destination addresses, the MAU acts as a logical ring with data packets traveling in sequence from node to node, as illustrated in Figure 11-3.

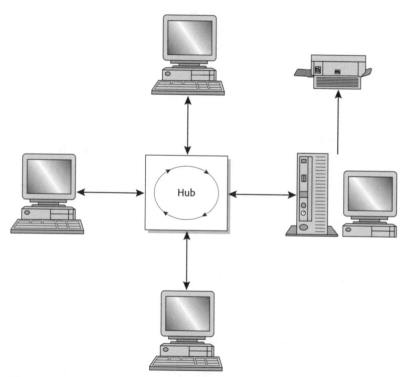

Figure 11-3 *Star-wired token ring network topology*

Star-wired token ring media access works this way: If data is to be sent by a computer at a network node, the node captures the token and attaches the data to the token, which, in turn, makes its status *busy*. Each consecutive node then checks the destination address of the data on the *busy* token to determine if it should process the data. It then passes the token on to the next node until the data reaches its destination where it is processed. When the transmission is complete, the data is stripped from the token, and its status is set back to *free*.

Defining Ethernet Architecture

Ethernet is the most common network architecture — which defines how computers, servers, and networking peripherals access the network cabling — and Ethernet employs an access method called Carrier Sense Multiple Access/Collision Detection (CSMA/CD). With these networks, each computer's Ethernet NIC, which uses a unique address called a Media Access Control (MAC) identification number, can sense a carrier signal on the network and refrains from transmitting data. If no carrier signal is detected, the NIC sends the data. If two or more NICs send data simultaneously, a collision occurs. The data collision is sensed by the other NICs and no data is sent until the collision has been resolved. After an arbitrary period of time, the original NICs that were involved with the data collision re-send their data packets.

With the CSMA/CD access control method, it is normal to have data collisions, provided that the number of collisions remain relatively low compared with the number of signals that transmit successfully.

Fast Ethernet networks use a different cable access method called Demand Priority Access (DPA). With DPA, a central hub controls access to the cable rather than the individual nodes. It also assigns a priority level to the data and ensures that the highest-priority data is sent along the network first.

Gigabit Ethernet retains the CSMA/CD and DPA media access control mechanisms and uses both twisted-pair and fiber cables. For these reasons, it is ideally suited for accessing server pipes, high-speed backbones, and connecting LANs to LANs.

Ethernet provides a maximum transmission rate of 10Mbps (Megabits per second), whereas Fast Ethernet supports a data throughput of 100Mbps, and Gigabit Ethernet supports up to a 1000Mbps transmission rate. Ethernet designs are governed by the IEEE Standard 802.3.

 KNOW THIS

Characteristics of Ethernet

For the A+ Core exam, you should know that Ethernet NICs use the CSMA/CD MAC method to access networks. You should also know what the maximum data transmission rates are:

- Ethernet: 10Mbps
- Fast Ethernet: 100Mbps
- Gigabit Ethernet: 1000Mbps

Identifying Network Cables and Connectors

Cables are the physical transmission media that connect the network devices together, serving as the conduit for information traveling from one computing device to another. Small networks employ only a single cable type, whereas large networks often use a combination of cable types, including twisted-pair, coaxial, and fiber-optic. Each cable type requires its own type of connector, such as the RJ-45, BNC, IBM data, and ST fiber-optic connectors. Table 11-1 presents Ethernet cable specifications.

Table 11-1 Ethernet Cable Specifications

Ethernet Cables	Media Type	Maximum Segment Length (Meters)	Maximum Number Nodes per Segment/ Link/Drop
10base-5	Thick coaxial (50-ohm, RJ-8)	500	100 per segment
10base-2	Thin coaxial (50-ohm, RJ-58)	185	30 per segment
10base-T	UTP (Cat. 5)	100	1 per link/drop
10base-F	Fiber-optic	2000	1 per link/drop

Half-Duplex versus Full-Duplex Data Transmission Modes

For the A+ Core exam, you should know that most networks use the half-duplex mode of data transmission. Networks transmit and receive data but not simultaneously. Modems and serial ports, on the other hand, use the full-duplex data transmission mode, meaning that they transmit and receive data simultaneously.

Twisted-Pair Cables

Twisted-pair is the most common type of network cable. It contains four pairs of insulated copper wires inside the same outer casing. Each pair is twisted with a different number of twists per inch. The wire twisting cancels out electrical noise and interference (called *crosstalk*) from adjacent wire pairs and from other electrical devices in the area. The two types of twisted-pair cable are unshielded twisted-pair (UTP) and shielded twisted-pair (STP).

Similar in appearance to telephone wire, UTP cabling is categorized from 1 to 5 according to the number of twists per inch. Category 5 UTP cable, which can transmit data up to 100Mbps, enables the fastest data transmission without crosstalk and provides the most reliable connections. UTP cables and RJ-45 connectors are used in Ethernet networks. Figure 11-4 illustrates a UTP cable.

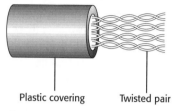

Plastic covering   Twisted pair

Figure 11-4 *An unshielded twisted-pair (UTP) cable*

When assembling RJ-45 connectors on UTP cables, a condition called *split pairs* can occur if the wire pairs are miswired. A *split pairs* condition reduces the bandwidth and causes frequent errors at the network node.

 Split pairs or miswired network connectors cause reduced bandwidth and frequent errors

STP cables not only use wire pair twisting to reduce crosstalk, but they also incorporate an intermediate-layered shield of woven copper braid and foil wrap to provide a high-degree of protection from outside electrical interference. STP cables are specified only for Token Ring LANs and use IBM data connectors. Figure 11-5 depicts a STP cable.

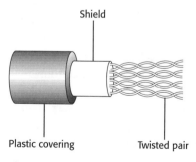

Shield

Plastic covering   Twisted pair

Figure 11-5 *A shielded twisted-pair (STP) cable*

Coaxial Cables

Coaxial cables have a copper wire surrounded by plastic insulation, a secondary braided copper conductor that acts as both a shield and a ground, and a plastic outside covering. Coaxial cables are available in two diameters: 0.4-inch (also called *thick coaxial* or 10base-5) and 0.2-inch (also called *thin coaxial* or 10base-2). Today, thin coaxial cable, which looks like television cable, is used exclusively in constructing networks, and requires BNC connectors. Figure 11-6 illustrates the coaxial cable.

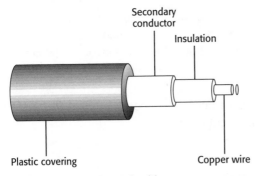

Figure 11-6 *A coaxial cable*

Fiber-Optic Cables

Fiber-optic cables contain two separate glass strands; each strand carries data in one direction. Each strand is surrounded by a reinforcing fiber material called Kevlar and is enclosed in a common plastic outside jacket. The glass strands carry pulses of light called *photons* that represent digital signals. The photons are unaffected by outside electromagnetic interference and do not radiate energy. Because they are free of electrical interference and capacitance, fiber-optic cables can carry high-speed signals over long distances. However, fiber-optic cables are much more expensive than copper cables. Figure 11-7 depicts a fiber-optic cable.

Special connectors (such as the ST fiber-optic connector) provide an optically pure interface connection between laser transmitters and optical receivers.

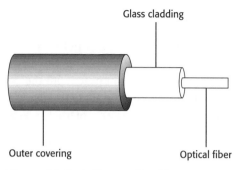

Glass cladding

Outer covering

Optical fiber

Figure 11-7 *A fiber-optic cable*

True or False?

1. 10base2 cable is also called thinnet or coaxial cable.

2. In a peer-to-peer network, all computers have basically equal status.

3. CSMA/CD is an acronym for Collision Sense Multiple Access/Collection Detection.

Answers: *1. True   2. True   3. False*

Defining Network Peripherals

The minimum hardware and software required to network computers and share services include Network Interface Cards, network cables and connectors, and a network operating system. However, depending on the network's topography and architecture, many other peripheral components must be considered in the network design.

Network Interface Cards

Network Interface Cards (NICs) connect the computer to LANs. NICs are installed in expansion slots on the system board, and provide two types of connections for the cables linking the computer with the Ethernet LAN. RJ-45 connectors are used to connect to twisted-pair cabling and Bayonet Naur Connector (BNC) connectors are used to connect to connect coaxial cabling.

There are two A+ Core exam questions that address Ethernet NIC configuration. One correct question and answer choice pair states that a computer is incapable of accessing the network if it is improperly configured. The other correct question and answer choice pair indicates that an electrically programmable read-only memory (EPROM) configuration switch can automatically set Interrupt-Requests (IRQs), precluding the need for jumpers or manual switches on the NIC.

Hubs

A hub (also called *a concentrator*) is the central meeting point for computer, server, and peripheral network cables in star and star-wired ring topology networks. It can contain from several to dozens of RJ-45 connecting ports or other connecting-type ports. Hubs can be either non-intelligent repeaters or intelligent network-traffic-management and control devices.

Bridges

A bridge is a peripheral device that connects two LANs or network segments together, providing both LANs use the same NOS. A bridge is often used to connect two segments of the same logical network when the number of nodes and amount of traffic have increased sufficiently and slow network performance. Dividing the overburdened network into segments improves network management and significantly increases the bandwidth.

Ethernet and Fast Ethernet Switches

A switch is a multi-port bridge that provides either a 10Mbps Ethernet or a 100Mbps Fast Ethernet connection between ports. Switches increase aggregate bandwidth dramatically by establishing simultaneous multiple connections. Switches also enable a high-bandwidth link to servers or backbones.

Routers

Routers, like bridges and switches, connect two or more physically separate network segments. However, unlike bridges and switches, which merely pass the data along the network, a router examines each data-packet address and determines the most efficient route between source and destination nodes. Routers are required for a LAN to access the Internet.

Gateways

Gateways are highly complex and powerful computers that link two or more networks with different network architectures and protocols. Gateways are required to access the Internet.

Understanding Network Protocols

As with formal diplomatic protocols that govern communications among nations, computer network protocols define how information is communicated among individual network devices, LANs, MANs, and WANs. The rules and standards that make up the network protocols ensure that the communication exchange flows smoothly and efficiently. The OSI Model is the design basis for numerous networking protocols, such as TCP/IP, IPX/SPX, and NetBEUI.

The Open System Interconnection Model

The Open System Interconnection (OSI) Model was developed by the International Standards Organization (ISO) in the late 1970s. The OSI Model defines a universal standard for designing data communication protocols so that equipment manufactured by companies can communicate. It is divided into seven layers that describe how information flows from one user to another. Each individual layer prepares information for and communicates with its contiguous layer. The lower layers are generally associated with hardware, whereas the upper layers are software dependent. Table 11-2 presents the OSI Model.

Table 11-2 Open System Interconnect Model

Layer	Title	Description
7	Application	Interfaces with operating system and supports user applications, such as e-mail, network management, file transfer, and database access
6	Presentation	Translates data to user-recognized languages and performs data compression, expansion, encryption and decryption
5	Session	Negotiates and establishes network node connections and controls when users send and receive data
4	Transport	Controls end-to-end data transmission
3	Network	Translates addresses and routes packets across networks
2	Data link	1) Logical Link Control (LCC): Transfers data frames, checks for errors, and provides data link services to higher layers
		2) Medium Access Control (MAC): Controls network access, such as CSMA/CD and token passing
1	Physical	Governs the design and properties of NICs and network cables/connectors

For the A+ Core exam question asking about the number of layers in the OSI Model, select the answer choice that references seven layers.

Transmission Control Protocol/Internet Protocol

In the early 1970s, the Department of Defense (DOD) established a set of networking protocols called TCP/IP, which is a suite of industry standards and agreements that define how data is transmitted across computer networks. TCP is the transport protocol and the IP is the network protocol in the OSI Model. TCP/IP is used in most UNIX operating systems (Windows 95, 98, NT, and 2000 provide built-in support) and provides the primary protocol on the Internet. For example, every host on a TCP/IP network is provided a unique IP address.

Internet Packet eXchange/ Sequenced Packet eXchange

Internet Packet eXchange/Sequenced Packet eXchange (IPX/SPX) is a protocol suite developed and maintained by Novell. The Microsoft version of IPX/SPX is called NetWare Link (NWLink). IPX is a connectionless network and transport layer protocol in the OSI Model that defines how to address and route data packets from one NetWare network to another. SPX is a connection-oriented extension of IPX involving the transport layer function in the OSI Model.

NetBIOS Extended User Interface

NetBIOS Extended User Interface (NetBEUI) is a small, very fast protocol that is used on small LANs. It is a combined network and transport layer protocol in the OSI Model developed by IBM and supported by Microsoft networks. Because it cannot route data packets, WANs do not use this non-routable protocol.

TCP/IP is the answer to the A+ Core exam question on which protocol is used on the Internet, and NetBEUI is the answer to the question on which protocol is used on Windows networks.

Have You Mastered?

Now it's time to review the concepts in this chapter and apply your knowledge. These questions test your mastery of the material covered in this chapter.

1. When referring to network cables, what does the acronym UTP stand for?

☐ A. Universal Tasking Procedures
☐ B. Unshielded twisted-pair
☐ C. Untied twin pair
☐ D. Universal tied pair

The correct answer is **B.** UTP is the acronym for unshielded twisted-pair cable. Refer to the "Identifying Network Cables and Connectors" section for more information.

2. Which type of network topology would generally use 10base2 cables and BNC connectors?

☐ A. Star
☐ B. Bus
☐ C. Token ring
☐ D. Star-wired token ring

The correct answer is **B.** Small bus topologies generally use 10base2 cables and BNC connectors. Refer to the "Understanding Network Topologies" section for more information.

3. Which type of LAN has the best user-level security?

☐ A. Peer-to-peer
☐ B. Client/server
☐ C. Bus
☐ D. Star

The correct answer is B. Client/server LANs provide excellent user-level security. Refer to the "Understanding Computer Networks" section for more information.

4. Which type of connector is used on a twisted-pair cable?

☐ A. RJ-45
☐ B. RJ-11
☐ C. BNC
☐ D. ST

The correct answer is A. RJ-45 connectors are used on twisted-pair cables. Refer to the "Identifying Network Cables and Connectors" section for more information.

5. In a full-duplex data transmission circuit, data travels in which direction?

☐ A. One direction only
☐ B. Both directions sequentially
☐ C. Both directions but not simultaneously
☐ D. Both directions simultaneously

The correct answer is D. Full-duplex circuits provide data travel in both directions simultaneously. Refer to the "Identifying Network Cables and Connectors" section for more information.

6. Which primary protocol is used on a Windows 95 network?

☐ A. IPX/SPX
☐ B. MS.25
☐ C. NetBEUI
☐ D. MS.125

The correct answer is **C**. Microsoft networks use the NetBEUI protocol. Refer to the "Understanding Network Protocols" section for more information.

7. How many layers are in the OSI network model?

- ☐ A. Seven
- ☐ B. Five
- ☐ C. Six
- ☐ D. Ten

The correct answer is **A**. The OSI Model contains seven layers. Refer to the "Understanding Network Protocols" section for more information.

8. Which types of network topologies use a point-to-point connection, linking all the computers to a central hub?

- ☐ A. Bus and MANs
- ☐ B. Fiber-optic and WANs
- ☐ C. Star and Star-wired token rings
- ☐ D. Backbone and LANs

The correct answer is **C**. Star and star-wired token ring networks use a point-to-point connection, linking all the computers to a central hub. Refer to the "Understanding Network Topologies" section for more information.

9. What is the maximum data transmission rate of the Fast Ethernet network architecture?

- ☐ A. 10Mbps
- ☐ B. 100Mbps
- ☐ C. 300Mbps
- ☐ D. 500Mbps

The correct answer is **B**. Maximum data transmission rate of the Fast Ethernet network is 100Mbps. Refer to the "Defining Ethernet Architecture" section for more information.

10. **Which networking peripheral device is generally used to connect two independent LANs with the same NOS?**

    ☐ A. A bridge
    ☐ B. A hub
    ☐ C. A concentrator
    ☐ D. A repeater

The correct answer is **A**. A bridge can be used to connect two independent LANs with the same NOS. Refer to the "Defining Network Peripherals" section for more information.

Total Customer Satisfaction

THIS CHAPTER ADDRESSES customer service and explains how good customer service contributes to total customer satisfaction. It prepares you to correctly answer A+ Core exam questions on effective communication skills, conflict resolution, and professional conduct. However, you should be aware that although the customer satisfaction domain is scored as part of the A+ Core exam, it does not count as part of your pass/fail grade.

Exam Material in This Chapter

Based on the Official Objectives

- Define customer satisfaction
- Contrast effective and ineffective customer service

Based on the Author's Experience

- Expect questions on communication and listening skills
- Be able to interpret verbal and non-verbal clues
- Know how to respond at the customer's technical level
- Understand how to establish a personal rapport with customers
- Prepare to answer questions on professional conduct
- Learn how to help and guide a customer describing a problem
- Understand how to avoid or resolve conflicts with customers

Are You Prepared?

Test your knowledge with the following questions. Then you'll know if you're prepared for the material in this chapter or if you should review problem areas.

1. **Over the telephone, an angry customer demands a replacement for a cable that he says has been defective since he bought his computer system from you, even though his system is no longer under warranty. What do you do?**

   ☐ A. Tell him to contact the cable manufacturer for a replacement.

   ☐ B. Tell him that you will send him a cable replacement immediately.

   ☐ C. Tell him that he must first have the cable tested to ensure that it is, in fact, defective, before you will consider replacing it.

   ☐ D. Tell him that he must purchase a new cable, regardless of what caused the defect because the system is no longer under warranty.

2. A customer complains that she has made numerous calls trying to contact you. She also says that because you have not responded, you must be avoiding talking with her. What do you do?

   ☐ A. Make the excuse that you're overworked.
   ☐ B. Agree that you are trying to avoid her because you really don't have the time to return her call.
   ☐ C. Apologize for the inconvenience and ask how you can help her.
   ☐ D. Give the customer to another service technician because you will, therefore, avoid future problems with her.

3. A customer is very upset and vents his frustration to you about how he can't boot his computer past the POST, and the fact that he has already spent many hours dealing with the problem. What is a good first step?

   ☐ A. Immediately clean off a work space and start diagnosing the computer problem to solve the customer's frustration as quickly as possible.
   ☐ B. Lay out your tools immediately, so that when he stops talking, you can get right to work.
   ☐ C. Ask him to stop talking because you cannot concentrate on solving the problem.
   ☐ D. Patiently wait for him to finish venting his frustration, then ask several questions that validate his feelings and elicit specific information about the problem.

Answers:

1. B   *The best approach is to resolve the situation quickly without furthering a customer's frustration. If possible, try to keep your customers happy. See the "Managing Conflicts" section.*

2. C   *Again, the best policy is to resolve the conflict quickly and keep the customer happy. See the "Managing Conflicts" section.*

3. D   *Effective listening skills are always helpful first steps when resolving problems. See the "Defining Communication Skills" section.*

Defining Total Customer Satisfaction

Customers are the people you depend on to purchase your products and services. Without them, you have no sales, no business, and no paycheck. You may interact with customers over the phone, in their home, or at your business. Regardless, ensuring total customer satisfaction is your primary job as a computer service professional.

Customers expect to receive a predefined or perceived level of service. When the actual service they receive comes as a surprise, customers generally evaluate it as either poor or excellent in comparison with their expectations. Your job as a computer service professional is not only to provide outstanding technical support, but also to furnish excellent customer service, which in turn grants total customer satisfaction.

Customer service excellence depends on your ability to communicate well and to establish a professional rapport with your customers. Speaking, writing, listening, body language, and conducting electronic interaction, such as telephone etiquette, are all forms of interpersonal communication. Establishing a professional rapport depends on your customer's impression of you and it often takes a long time to develop. However, remember, you get only one chance to make a good first impression.

Total Customer Satisfaction

For the A+ Core exam, outstanding technical support (OTS) plus excellent customer service (ECS) equals total customer satisfaction (TCS); that is, OTS + ECS = TCS. Also know that a computer service professional is expected to employ effective interpersonal communication skills, such as speaking, writing, listening, and using proper telephone etiquette.

Establishing Customer Contacts

Although it seems unfair, prospective customers often form lasting impressions immediately based on simple actions. How many rings it takes you to answer the phone, or whether or not you smile and have a positive attitude can shape a customer's image of you. As a service professional, you must be prepared to handle initial customer contacts gracefully.

Preparing for the Service Call

Before you contact customers or travel to a site to provide service, review the customer's service history, evaluate the sense of urgency and the level of priority. Assemble the appropriate tool and parts kit. Be realistic about scheduling the appointment, and notify the customer quickly if you cannot keep the agreed-upon appointment. Above all else, be on time for your appointments. Other tips for preparing for service calls are:

- Anticipate problems that can arise during the call.
- Use a checklist to ensure nothing is forgotten.
- Take more than enough parts and tools than are required.

Establishing Customer Rapport

It is important to establish your credibility early. Make eye contact, maintain good body posture, and remain calm and confident. Learn the customer's name and use it often in your discussions. Be friendly, approachable, polite, and respectful. Once you have demonstrated your technical expertise by resolving the customer's problems, you are well on your way to total customer satisfaction. Other guidelines to establish customer rapport are as follows:

- Respect the customer's opinions (observe the old adage "The customer is always right") and respect the customer's time constraints.

- When a customer complains, attempt not to be defensive or to take criticisms personally.
- Extend options if the customer's initial expectations cannot be met.

Identifying Your Customer's Technical Knowledge Level

Determine your customer's technical abilities and knowledge, and adjust your conversation accordingly. Avoid technical jargon, and explain your terminology if you feel it may be misunderstood. And if the customer is obviously computer illiterate, ask simple yes or no questions. Other communication tips with regard to your customer's level of technical expertise are as follows:

- Never belittle your customer because of his or her limited technical knowledge or expertise.
- Use your knowledge to solve problems and not for personal gain or power over your customers.
- Teach your customers so they can help themselves later.

Service Call Preparation

For the A+ Core exam, you should know the following about service call preparation: First review the customer's service history, evaluate the sense of urgency involved, and the level of priority. Then assemble a tool and parts kit tailored for the specific service call. Above all else, don't be late for the appointment.

Defining Communication Skills

Communicating effectively and clearly is one of the most important skills for customer service personnel. For example, how do you determine your customers' needs or wants? Although you may simply ask them, there is more to effective communication than just speaking.

Listen Actively

Active listening means allowing customers to speak without interruption and permitting them to completely express their thoughts before you ask questions. Active listening enables a service professional not only to hear what customers are saying, but also to extract important information and clues from the conversation, especially about problem symptoms or data that may help resolve problems or situations. Active listening also means picking up on non-verbal communication, such as a smile or a scowl. Does the facial message match the verbal message, or does body language reveal more than is said?

Rephrase Statements and Questions

A customer may convey a different message than the one that he or she intended. Rephrasing a statement validates that what you think you heard is, in fact, what was said. Asking the customer, "for the sake of clarity, let me repeat what I just thought you said," and then rephrasing the customer's statement or question in your own words is an example of rephrasing.

Ask Questions

In the course of a discussion, ask questions and actively listen to the answers. Customers may provide only general information when you are looking for specific information related to individual problems or situations, so ask questions to uncover these details.

Speak Slowly, Calmly, and Clearly

Verbal communication can be only as effective as the manner in which it is delivered. If you have a tendency to speak too fast, slow down. Everyone tends to speak more quickly when excited, so remain calm. Other important speech factors to consider are your voice inflections, which are changes in pitch or tone highs and lows, your volume, and your enunciation.

Additionally, watch for the customer's non-verbal communication, facial expressions and body language, for clues about how he or she may be reacting to you or the situation.

Finally, be aware of your word choice, especially when it involves technical words or jargon.

Use Non-Verbal Communication

Studies on how people interpret messages from other people indicate that people receive messages based on the following factors, in order of how effective each is:

1. Body language
2. Tone of voice
3. Meaning of words

The primary elements of non-verbal communication or body language are as follows:

- Extending a firm, but not overbearing, handshake
- Maintaining proper eye contact
- Setting a positive tone using facial expressions
- Keeping culturally correct physical distances between persons
- Using proper hand gestures for emphasis
- Facing in the customer's direction
- Nodding or leaning forward to make a point

 TEST TIP Fact finding or asking questions about operating events that have occurred prior to a problem with a computer is an essential step in fault-diagnostics. The communication skills that you can employ to question the customer about the computer's history include speaking, active listening, and rephrasing of statements or questions.

Understanding Professional Telephone Support

The telephone is often the first contact and impression that prospective customers have with you and your company. Exercising proper telephone etiquette is an easy way for a customer to make an immediate positive impression of you and your company.

Answering the Telephone

First, you should always attempt to answer the telephone within thee rings. Any longer and the customer may think that either you don't care about his or her call or that your company is understaffed and doesn't have enough people to answer the phones.

Second, you should answer each call with an appropriate greeting. Begin by saying, "Hello, good morning," or "Hello, good afternoon," in a professional manner and then identify yourself or your company.

When you ask, "How may I help you?" you have completed the greeting segment of the customer's call.

Listening Carefully

It is important that you employ active listening right away. Listen carefully to what the customer says, and then ask questions or rephrase the customer's statements to extract additional detailed information. Also, take notes to ensure you remember the details.

Transferring Calls

Transferring a customer among multiple employees is an easy way to make a bad impression. Again, the customer may assume that you don't care about him or her or that you're too busy. Always ask the customer if he or she minds being transferred before actually transferring the call.

Additionally, ensure that someone is available to pick up the call and inform the customer of that person's identity prior to making the transfer.

Placing the Customer on Hold

Because placing customers on hold is an inconvenience, always ask their permission. Tell a customer why you're placing him or her on hold and estimate a time frame for his or her wait. Then, after returning to the line, thank the customer for his or her patience.

Ending the Conversation

At the end of the conversation, thank your customer for the call and allow him or her to hang up first. Then immediately record key information about the conversation before becoming distracted by another call or activity.

Select the A+ Core exam answer choice that is similar to the following sequence of events: Tom Hardy, a computer service professional, answers the phone within three rings. He then says, "Hello, good morning, this is Tom Hardy (or he may use his company's name), may I help you?" After conducting business, Tom ends the conversation by allowing the customer to hang up first and then he records important information about the call before he forgets or becomes distracted.

Managing Conflicts

Inevitably, situations get out of hand and result in conflict. And whatever tactic you take, you are unable to prevent your customer from becoming angry. Typical examples of reasons why service customers may become upset or angry follow:

- The customer is treated rudely or unprofessionally
- The customer is not pleased with the product or services

- The customer is given incorrect information
- Specific deadlines are missed or orders are filled incorrectly

The easiest way to handle conflicts is to remain calm and let the customer vent his or her anger without initially replying. Never tell an angry customer to calm down because it only elevates his or her anger. Empathize with the customer about the problem or situation, and then redirect the conversation into positive channels, creating solutions to the causes of the conflict. End the conflict in the customer's favor, if possible.

TEST TIP

The more effective and easiest way to handle a conflict is to remain calm and permit the customer to vent his or her anger. Then resolve the conflict in the customer's favor, if possible.

You also must recognize that not everything that customers may want is possible. Rather than getting angry and creating a conflict, a reasonable customer may simply be disappointed. You may have to say no to customers for the following reasons:

- Legal and/or federal or state regulations
- Company policies
- The product is not in stock
- It is impossible to accommodate the customer

Apply the same conflict resolution strategy to resolving a customer's disappointment, but also emphasize the options or alternatives to the situation.

Understanding Professional Conduct

Many companies post a service professional's code of conduct. You should also have your own code of conduct, which includes the following rules:

- Maintain a clean, neat, personal appearance and wear appropriate attire

- Be responsive to the customer's sense of urgency
- Promise less, deliver more
- Be accountable for resolving the total situation
- Provide options to resolve impasses
- Complete the entire job, including testing
- Avoid distracting employees at the work site
- Follow up on unresolved issues
- Complete the paperwork
- Maintain an orderly workspace
- Maintain an appropriate parts inventory

Have You Mastered?

Now it's time to review the concepts in this chapter and apply your knowledge. These questions test your mastery of the material covered in this chapter.

1. **A customer calls and states that your delivery truck has just dropped off his repaired computer and the power cord is missing. What do you do?**

   ☐ A. Offer to send him a power cord through the mail.

   ☐ B. Immediately order a power cord from the manufacturer and have it drop-shipped to your customer's address.

   ☐ C. Tell him that you will have the delivery truck drop off a cable immediately.

   ☐ D. Tell him that it's not your problem because you double-checked his computer before delivery, and that you're sure a power cable was part of the system.

   The correct answer is **C**. The best policy is to resolve problems or situations quickly and, if possible, in the customer's favor. Refer to the "Managing Conflicts" section for more information.

2. An irate customer calls and states that the computer you just serviced still does not operate properly, and she needs to do her taxes on a computer right away. What do you do?

☐ A. Tell her to take it to another service facility because you're just too busy to help her right now.

☐ B. Offer to fix it again, but tell her she will have to wait several days to pick it up.

☐ C. Offer to re-service her computer and loan her a temporary computer.

☐ D. Let her vent her anger, then try to talk her through the problem step-by-step. If that doesn't work, have her bring the computer into your service facility.

The correct answer is C. Re-servicing her computer and loaning her another computer in the meantime resolves her major concern about getting her work done immediately. Refer to the "Managing Conflicts" section for more information.

3. A customer has difficulty explaining a computer problem during a telephone conversation with you. What do you do?

☐ A. Tell him to bring the computer into your service facility because you don't know what he's talking about.

☐ B. Be patient and ask easy yes or no questions to obtain specific information about the problem.

☐ C. Ask for someone else to explain the problem because you don't know what he's talking about.

☐ D. Have another service technician get on the phone to see if he or she can understand what the customer is saying.

The correct answer is B. Asking questions can play a big part in gathering information to resolve problems quickly. Refer to the "Defining Communication Skills" section for more information.

4. A customer complains that he has been transferred five times and wants a response to his questions or he'll take his business elsewhere. What do you do?

☐ A. Tell him that everyone is extremely busy and you'll have to return his call later.

☐ B. Ask for the names of the employees he had previously spoken with and tell him you'll report them to the boss.

☐ C. Apologize for the inconvenience and answer his questions.

☐ D. Transfer him to another employee to avoid any more unpleasantness.

The correct answer is C. The best approach is to apologize for the inconvenience and answer his question(s). Refer to the "Defining Communication Skills" section for more information.

5. A customer is angry and complains that an employee in your company has been rude and obnoxious to him. What do you do?

☐ A. Tell him that you'll take the complaint to management, then ask how you can help him.

☐ B. Let him vent his anger, apologize on behalf of the company, and then ask how you can help him.

☐ C. Tell him that there is nothing that you can do about it, but ask how you can help him.

☐ D. Try to talk him out of his complaint, then ask how you can help him.

The correct answer is B. The best and easiest approach to this problem is to let the customer vent his anger, to apologize on behalf of the company, and then ask how you can help him. Refer to the "Managing Conflicts" section for more information.

6. Within how many rings should you answer the telephone?

☐ A. Two
☐ B. Three
☐ C. Four
☐ D. Five

The correct answer is B. Answer the telephone within three rings. Refer to the "Understanding Professional Telephone Support " section for more information.

7. **What is the best procedure to use when answering the phone?**

   ☐ A. Give the company name and ask "Who's calling?"
   ☐ B. Identify yourself and ask "Who's calling, please?"
   ☐ C. Say, "Hello, good morning," identify yourself or your company, and ask "How can I help you?"
   ☐ D. Say, "Hello," then identify your company.

The correct answer is C. Saying, "Hello, good morning," or "Hello, good afternoon," identifying yourself or your company, and then asking, "How can I help you?" is the best telephone answering etiquette. Refer to the "Understanding Professional Telephone Support" section for more information.

8. **How should you prepare for an on-site service call, in addition to ensuring that you have the customer's name, address, and telephone number?**

   ☐ A. Review the problem description, the customer's service history, the sense of urgency, and the level of priority. Then assemble the appropriate tool and parts kit based on the problem description.
   ☐ B. Review the problem description, and than simply assume that you have enough parts and tools for any service call.
   ☐ C. Assume that your parts and tool kit is assembled and ready to go. You probably will bring the computer back for repair, anyway.
   ☐ D. Assemble one of every computer component or part that you assume you'll need, and get your tool kit ready to go.

The correct answer is **A**. To prepare for a service call, review the problem description, the customer's service history, the sense of urgency, and the level of priority. Then assemble the appropriate tool and parts kit for the service call. Refer to the "Establishing Customer Contacts" section for more information.

9. How should you respond to a customer who is obviously computer illiterate?

☐ A. Ask easy-to-answer yes or no questions.
☐ B. Avoid computer terminology or technical jargon.
☐ C. Avoid embarrassing him or her.
☐ D. All of the above.

The correct answer is **D**. All of the answers are correct. Refer to the "Establishing Customer Contacts" section for more information.

10. What is the primary goal of a service call?

☐ A. To repair equipment
☐ B. To provide total customer satisfaction
☐ C. To solve problems
☐ D. To contribute to the company's profit

The correct answer is **B**. The primary goal of a service call is to provide total customer satisfaction, which is equal to outstanding technical service plus excellent customer service. Refer to the "Defining Total Customer Satisfaction" section for more information.

Exam & Analysis

Practice Exam

1. Which of the following is not stored in the ROM BIOS?

☐ A. POST
☐ B. CMOS Setup
☐ C. Bootstrap loader
☐ D. CMOS

2. POST does not test which of the following?

☐ A. The power supply
☐ B. The RAM
☐ C. The keyboard
☐ D. The video adapter card

3. Which of the following voltages is not supplied by the power supply?

☐ A. – 12 volts
☐ B. + 12 volts
☐ C. + 9 volts
☐ D. – 5 volts

4. How many conductors are contained in a narrow SCSI-2 cable?

☐ A. 68
☐ B. 50
☐ C. 34
☐ D. 40

5. Which port uses a male 9-pin (DB9) connector?

☐ A. Parallel
☐ B. SCSI
☐ C. Game
☐ D. Serial

6. How many pins are contained in an EIDE connector?

☐ A. 40
☐ B. 34
☐ C. 50
☐ D. 25

7. Which type of connector is used to connect a modem to a telephone line?

☐ A. RJ-45
☐ B. RJ-11
☐ C. BNC
☐ D. DB9

8. What does a red stripe on the edge of a ribbon cable indicate?

☐ A. It has no meaning.
☐ B. It is the manufacturer's code.
☐ C. Pin 1.
☐ D. The highest pin number.

9. **How many individual hard disk drives can be installed on the secondary EIDE channel?**

   ☐ A. 2
   ☐ B. 4
   ☐ C. 5
   ☐ D. 3

10. **What is the maximum number of SCSI devices that can be attached to a Fast/Wide SCSI-3 bus?**

    ☐ A. 16
    ☐ B. 15
    ☐ C. 7
    ☐ D. 8

11. **IRQs enable a hardware device to perform which of the following?**

    ☐ A. Move blocks of data directly into memory
    ☐ B. To be assigned an I/O port number
    ☐ C. Alert the CPU that the hardware device needs attention
    ☐ D. Reserve an address in memory

12. **How many conductors are contained in a floppy disk drive ribbon cable?**

    ☐ A. 34
    ☐ B. 30
    ☐ C. 40
    ☐ D. 50

13. **What is the primary advantage to Flash BIOS?**

    ☐ A. It uses less power
    ☐ B. It is faster than older ROM
    ☐ C. It can be updated without disassembling the computer
    ☐ D. It includes CMOS

14. Which of the following is not a hard disk drive industry design standard?

☐ A. IDE
☐ B. EIDE
☐ C. SCSI
☐ D. EISA

15. What is the default IRQ setting assignment for COM4?

☐ A. 3
☐ B. 2
☐ C. 5
☐ D. 7

16. Which device can be connected to an RS-232C serial port?

☐ A. The keyboard
☐ B. The printer
☐ C. The external modem
☐ D. The monitor

17. What is the primary purpose of a modem?

☐ A. To convert analog to digital signals and vice versa
☐ B. To amplify signals
☐ C. To convert positive to negative power and vice versa
☐ D. To convert serial into parallel communications and vice versa

18. What type of connector is used on a Network Interface Card?

☐ A. RJ-11
☐ B. RJ-45
☐ C. DB9
☐ D. DB5

19. Which of the following is not a valid SCSI connector?

- ☐ A. DB25
- ☐ B. 68-pin connector
- ☐ C. 50-pin connector
- ☐ D. 36-pin Centronix

20. What is the default IRQ setting assignment for LPT1?

- ☐ A. 5
- ☐ B. 7
- ☐ C. 12
- ☐ D. 2

21. How are two hard disk drives configured on a secondary EIDE channel?

- ☐ A. Primary/secondary
- ☐ B. First/second
- ☐ C. Master/slave
- ☐ D. Single/dual

22. What is the resistance of a fuse rated at 10 amps @ 150 volts that has not been blown?

- ☐ A. Infinite ohms
- ☐ B. < 1 ohm
- ☐ C. 15 ohms
- ☐ D. 1500 ohms

23. What multimeter selection is the best to use when checking the power at a wall outlet?

- ☐ A. 100 volts AC range
- ☐ B. 200 volts DC range
- ☐ C. 1000 volts AC range
- ☐ D. 200 volts AC range

24. **A parity error is a symptom of which of the following?**

    ☐ A. Defective SIMM
    ☐ B. Defective CPU
    ☐ C. Defective BIOS
    ☐ D. Defective RTC/CMOS chip

25. **If the real-time clock is losing time, the problem is probably due to:**

    ☐ A. A defective system clock
    ☐ B. The low voltage state of the BIOS battery
    ☐ C. The low voltage state of the RTC/CMOS battery
    ☐ D. A defective operating system

26. **An indication of an ATX-class power supply failure could be which of the following?**

    ☐ A. + 11.6 volt output
    ☐ B. + and – 5 volt output
    ☐ C. + 3.3 volt output
    ☐ D. No fan rotation

27. **Which of the following causes a single beep during startup?**

    ☐ A. The POST has discovered no errors
    ☐ B. A missing keyboard
    ☐ C. A BIOS problem
    ☐ D. The CPU failure

28. **Missing slot plates or other openings in the system unit case probably cause which of the following to occur?**

    ☐ A. EMI radiation
    ☐ B. The system runs too cold
    ☐ C. The system runs too hot
    ☐ D. It has no effect

29. **During modem installation, a conflict occurs between the new modem and another device. What is the most likely cause of the conflict?**

    ☐ A. IRQ conflict
    ☐ B. DMA conflict
    ☐ C. Defective modem
    ☐ D. I/O address conflict

30. **What tool or instrument is most likely used to troubleshoot serial and parallel ports?**

    ☐ A. A logic probe
    ☐ B. A multimeter
    ☐ C. A continuity meter
    ☐ D. A loopback connector

31. **Which symptom is not identified by POST during boot?**

    ☐ A. RAM that becomes defective at elevated temperatures
    ☐ B. A defective keyboard
    ☐ C. An inoperative ROM BIOS chip
    ☐ D. A defective system board (motherboard)

32. **Following hard disk drive replacement, the *fixed disk error* on-screen message appears during boot. How do you resolve the problem?**

    ☐ A. Run FDISK
    ☐ B. Run FORMAT
    ☐ C. Run the Setup program and change the drive's settings in CMOS
    ☐ D. Reinstall DOS

33. Following hard disk drive replacement, the *invalid media type* on-screen error message appears during boot. How do you resolve the problem?

☐ A. Run FDISK

☐ B. Run FORMAT

☐ C. Run the Setup program and change the CMOS settings

☐ D. Reinstall DOS

34. Which of the following most likely causes a CPU overheating problem?

☐ A. A power supply fan failure

☐ B. A power supply providing too much voltage

☐ C. CPU fan failure

☐ D. Too many hardware devices loading the CPU

35. When cleaning circuit boards, what is the first task to perform?

☐ A. Tap the board sharply to dislodge debris

☐ B. Blow dust away

☐ C. Clean the board with a sponge

☐ D. Reseat the socket chips

36. Which of the following does not require special disposal?

☐ A. CRT

☐ B. Laser toner cartridge

☐ C. Batteries

☐ D. Chemical cleaning solutions

37. When should you not wear an anti-static wrist strap?

☐ A. Replacing a CPU

☐ B. Replacing a RAM

☐ C. Working on a CRT

☐ D. Working on a system board

38. What does the acronym MSDS mean?

- [ ] A. Microsoft System Design Specification
- [ ] B. Material Safety Data Sheet
- [ ] C. Master System Design Specification
- [ ] D. Material System Design Specification

39. Which of the following materials reduce ESD problems?

- [ ] A. Rubber
- [ ] B. Nylon
- [ ] C. Plastic
- [ ] D. Vinyl

40. When is ESD potential highest?

- [ ] A. High humidity
- [ ] B. Low humidity
- [ ] C. Warm moist air
- [ ] D. During an electrical storm

41. Which fire extinguisher rating is used only for electrical fires?

- [ ] A. A
- [ ] B. B
- [ ] C. C
- [ ] D. ABC

42. A DIMM memory module contains how many pins?

- [ ] A. 30
- [ ] B. 168
- [ ] C. 128
- [ ] D. 72

43. What is the memory capacity of a 4M × 32 SIMM memory module?

    ☐ A. 32MB
    ☐ B. 16MB
    ☐ C. 128MB
    ☐ D. 64MB

44. Which class of system boards uses a *soft power switch* to shutdown the computer?

    ☐ A. XT
    ☐ B. ATX
    ☐ C. AT
    ☐ D. EIDE

45. What does the CMOS contain?

    ☐ A. CMOS Setup program
    ☐ B. BIOS
    ☐ C. POST
    ☐ D. Device configuration settings

46. Which socket or slot is used with a Pentium II processor?

    ☐ A. Socket 7
    ☐ B. Slot 1
    ☐ C. Socket 5
    ☐ D. Socket 8

47. What voltage supply is required for a 486 processor with the exception of a 486DX4?

    ☐ A. 5 volts
    ☐ B. 3.3 volts
    ☐ C. 10 volts
    ☐ D. 7.5 volts

48. What is the available L2 cache size for 686 processors?

☐ A. 128K and 512K
☐ B. 256K and 512K
☐ C. 64K and 128K
☐ D. 128K and 256K

49. If a laser printer passes self-test and still does not print, what is the next item to check?

☐ A. The fuser pads
☐ B. The discharge comb
☐ C. The laser assembly
☐ D. The interface connections between printer and host

50. In a laser printer, the thermal fuse (thermostat) is used to prevent which of the following?

☐ A. The fuser assembly from overheating
☐ B. The high-voltage power supply from overheating
☐ C. The laser from overheating
☐ D. The drum from overheating

51. What causes a laser printer to print totally black pages?

☐ A. A thermal switch in the fuser assembly malfunction
☐ B. A defective transfer corona wire
☐ C. A defective laser scanner assembly
☐ D. A defective primary corona wire

52. What causes an impact printer to slow down after heavy use?

☐ A. The thermal protection circuit in the print head is functioning properly.
☐ B. Friction causes the mechanical parts to stick.
☐ C. The motor assembly cannot handle the load.
☐ D. The power supply is not keeping up with the electrical load.

53. What usually causes multiple sheets to be pulled simultaneously from the paper tray in a laser printer?

☐ A. The paper is too thick.
☐ B. The paper is too tightly packed.
☐ C. The paper has too much moisture.
☐ D. The paper is the wrong type.

54. Which of the following is *not* a reason to exercise caution when working on a laser printer?

☐ A. The laser beam can cause severe eye damage
☐ B. Voltage can build to -6000 volts
☐ C. The toner is dangerous if you touch it
☐ D. The drum can contain a -600 volt charge

55. Which type of PC-Card (PCMCIA) Slot in a portable computer supports a hard drive?

☐ A. Type III
☐ B. Type I
☐ C. Type II
☐ D. Type IV

56. What must first be performed in a portable computer before it can recognize PC Cards?

☐ A. The software enabler must be installed
☐ B. COM4 must be enabled
☐ C. The PCMCIA operator must be installed
☐ D. COM2 must be enabled

57. What type of batteries can be used to replace NiCad batteries in a portable computer?

☐ A. Li-Ion
☐ B. NiMH
☐ C. NiCad only
☐ D. MXnx

58. The primary advantage active matrix displays have over passive matrix displays is that active matrix displays are:

    ☐ A. Brighter
    ☐ B. Larger
    ☐ C. Use less power
    ☐ D. Less expensive

59. In a full-duplex communication circuit, data travels in which direction?

    ☐ A. One direction only
    ☐ B. Both directions but not simultaneously
    ☐ C. Both directions simultaneously
    ☐ D. Both directions sequentially

60. An improperly configured NIC can cause the following problem:

    ☐ A. Prevent the computer from starting up
    ☐ B. Prevent network access
    ☐ C. Damage other cards
    ☐ D. Cause power supply failure

61. When configuring an ISA NIC without jumpers or PnP, what sets the IRQ?

    ☐ A. CMOS
    ☐ B. DMA
    ☐ C. BIOS
    ☐ D. EPROM configuration switch

62. What is the MAC method used by Ethernet called?

    ☐ A. Token Ring
    ☐ B. UTP
    ☐ C. CSMA/CD
    ☐ D. IPX/SPX

63. On a Windows network, what is the primary protocol?

- ☐ A. NetBIOS
- ☐ B. NetBEUI
- ☐ C. IPX/SPX
- ☐ D. TCP/IP

64. While discussing a problem with a customer over the telephone, she demands a replacement for a cable she states is defective. What do you do?

- ☐ A. Tell her to contact the cable manufacturer for a replacement
- ☐ B. Tell her that you will send her a replacement
- ☐ C. Tell her that she must first test the cable to ensure that it is defective, then you will replace it
- ☐ D. Hang up because she is acting unreasonably

65. A customer complains that he has made numerous attempts to contact you, but you never respond and seem to be avoiding him. What do you do?

- ☐ A. Make the excuse that you're overworked
- ☐ B. Agree that you are avoiding him
- ☐ C. Apologize for the inconvenience and ask how you can help him
- ☐ D. Give the customer to another service technician

Exam Key

1. D	26. D	51. D
2. A	27. A	52. A
3. C	28. C	53. B
4. B	29. A	54. C
5. D	30. D	55. A
6. A	31. A	56. A
7. B	32. C	57. B
8. C	33. B	58. A
9. A	34. C	59. C
10. B	35. D	60. B
11. C	36. B	61. D
12. A	37. C	62. C
13. C	38. B	63. B
14. D	39. A	64. B
15. A	40. B	65. C
16. C	41. C	
17. A	42. B	
18. B	43. B	
19. D	44. B	
20. B	45. D	
21. C	46. B	
22. B	47. A	
23. D	48. B	
24. A	49. D	
25. C	50. A	

Exam Analysis

1. The answer is **D.** The POST, CMOS Setup, and bootstrap loader are part of the BIOS, which is encoded on the ROM chip. CMOS, on the other hand, is contained on the RTC chip. For more on this subject, see the "Understanding the ROM BIOS Chip" section in Chapter 4.

2. The answer is **A.** Power supplies check their own operational readiness during computer boot instead of relying on the POST. A Power_Good signal indicates that the power supply does not have a problem and that it is ready to supply power to the various hardware devices. For more on this subject, see the "Power Supplies" section in Chapter 1.

3. The answer is **C.** Power supplies do not provide + 9 volts because no devices require this voltage. For more on this subject, see the "Power Supplies" section in Chapter 1.

4. The answer is **B.** Narrow SCSI-2 cables contain 50 conductors, whereas SCSI-3 cables contain 68. For more on this subject, see the "Understanding the Small Computer System Interface Bus" section in Chapter 3.

5. The answer is **D.** Serial I/O ports use either male 9-pin (DB9) or male 25-pin (DB25). For more on this subject, see the "Understanding I/O Ports and Identifying Back Panel Connectors" section in Chapter 3.

6. The answer is **A.** Both IDE and EIDE connectors contain 40 pins. For more on this subject see the "Hard Disk Drive System Interface Standards" section in Chapter 7.

7. The answer is **B.** Modems use RJ-11 connectors to connect to telephone lines. For more on this subject, see the "Communication and Network Connectors" section in Chapter 3.

8. The answer is **C.** A red stripe along the edge of a ribbon cable indicates pin 1. For more on this subject, see the "Reassembling the System Unit Case" section in Chapter 2.

9. The answer is **A.** Two individual hard disk drives can be installed on the secondary EIDE channel. For more on this subject, see the "Hard Disk Drive System Interface Standards" section in Chapter 7.

10. The answer is **B.** Up to 15 SCSI devices can be installed on a Fast Wide SCSI-3 bus. For more on this subject, see the "Understanding the Small Computer System Interface Bus" section in Chapter 3.

11. The answer is **C.** An IRQ alerts the CPU that the hardware device needs attention. For more on this subject, see the "Understanding PC Communication Pathways" section in Chapter 8.

12. The answer is **A.** A floppy disk drive ribbon cable contains 34 conductors. For more on this subject, see the "Replacing Floppy Disk Drives" section in Chapter 7.

13. The answer is **C.** Flash BIOS can be upgraded using software and precludes disassembling the computer. For more on this subject, see the "Understanding the ROM BIOS Chip" section in Chapter 4.

14. The answer is **D.** IDE, EIDE, and SCSI are hard disk drive industry design standards, whereas EISA is a system bus design standard. For more on this subject, see the "Understanding System Bus Architectures" section in Chapter 4.

15. The answer is **A.** The default IRQ setting assignment for COM4 is IRQ3. For more on this subject, see the "Understanding PC Communication Pathways" section in Chapter 8.

16. The answer is **C.** Because modems communicate serially, they are usually connected to RS-232C serial ports. For more on this subject, see the "Understanding I/O Ports and Identifying Back Panel Connectors" section in Chapter 3.

17. The answer is **A.** A modem converts analog to digital signals and vice versa. For more on this subject, see the "Recognizing System Unit Case Features" section in Chapter 3.

18. The answer is **B.** A RJ-45 connector is used on an NIC to connect it to a network over 10baseT wire. For more on this subject, see the "Defining Ethernet Architecture" section in Chapter 11.

19. The answer is **D.** DB25, 50-pin and 68-pin connectors are used on SCSI buses, whereas a 36-pin Centronix connector is used on a parallel printer. For more on this subject, see the "Understanding the Small Computer System Interface Bus" section in Chapter 3.

20. The answer is **B.** The default IRQ setting assignment is IRQ7. For more on this subject, see the "Understanding PC Communication Pathways" section in Chapter 8.

21. The answer is **C.** Two hard disk drives are configured in a master/slave arrangement when installed on a secondary EIDE channel. For more on this subject, see the "Hard Disk Drive System Interface Standards" section in Chapter 7.

22. The answer is **B.** A functional fuse's resistance is less than one ohm. For more on this subject, see the "Assembling a Basic Servicing Tool Kit" section in Chapter 2.

23. The answer is **D.** The multimeter should be set on the 200 volts AC range because the power at a wall outlet is nominally 117 volts AC. For more on this subject, see the "Assembling a Basic Servicing Tool Kit" section in Chapter 2.

24. The answer is **A.** A parity error is a symptom of a defective SIMM. For more on this subject, see the "Understanding Parity Error Checking" section in Chapter 6.

25. The answer is **C.** Losing time is the first symptom of an RTC/CMOS battery problem and the battery should be replaced immediately. For more on this subject, see the "Understanding the ROM BIOS Chip" section in Chapter 4.

26. The answer is **D.** If the fan is not rotating, it is likely the power supply is defective and should be replaced. For more on this subject, see the "Maintaining CPU Reliability" section in Chapter 5.

27. The answer is **A.** A single beep during startup indicates that the POST has discovered no errors. For more on this subject, see the "Identifying FRUs Inside the System Unit Case" section in Chapter 1.

28. The answer is **C.** Missing slot plates can cause the system to run too hot. For more on this subject, see the "Disassembling the System Unit Case" section in Chapter 2.

29. The answer is **A.** Conflicting IRQ setting assignments are often the cause of problems during installation of new devices. For more on this subject, see the "Understanding PC Communication Pathways" section in Chapter 8.

30. The answer is **D.** A loopback connector is used to troubleshoot serial and parallel ports. For more on this subject, see the "Assembling a Basic Servicing Tool Kit" section in Chapter 2.

31. The answer is **A.** POST is performed during startup before the internal temperature has risen causing a RAM problem. For more on this subject, see the "Understanding the ROM BIOS Chip" section in Chapter 4.

32. The answer is **C.** An incorrect CMOS setting will cause a *fixed disk error* on-screen message. Run the Setup program and change the drive's configuration settings in CMOS. For more on this subject, see the "Hard Disk Drive System Interface Standards" section in Chapter 7.

33. The answer is **B.** An improperly formatted hard disk will cause an "invalid media type" on-screen message. Run FORMAT to reformat the drive. For more on this subject, see the "Hard Disk Drive System Interface Standards" section in Chapter 7.

34. The answer is **C.** Intel 486 and newer CPUs have a cooling fan, and they will often fail if the fan becomes defective. For more on this subject, see the "Maintaining CPU Reliability" section in Chapter 5.

35. The answer is **D.** Before blowing debris off a circuit board using compressed air, the socket chips should be seated. The reason for this is that dust particles may get on the exposed connectors and cause a poor connection when reseated. For more on this subject, see the "Disassembling the System Unit Case" section in Chapter 2.

36. The answer is **B.** Laser toner cartridges do not require special disposal, whereas CRTs, batteries, and chemical cleaning solutions must be disposed of in accordance with the local EPA or the item's MSDS. For more on this subject, see the "Identifying Special Servicing Concerns" section in Chapter 2.

37. The answer is **C.** Never wear an anti-static wrist strap when servicing a CRT because it can generate up to 25,000 volts at the anode. The wrist strap can provide a direct ground path for the current to travel through your body to ground. For more on this subject, see the "Protecting Service Personnel from Electrical Shock and Laser Beams" section in Chapter 2.

38. The answer is **B.** MSDS is an acronym for Material Safety Data Sheet. MSDSs are provided by manufacturers and are required by law to assist in establishing safety and disposal guidelines. For more on this subject, see the "Identifying Special Servicing Concerns" section in Chapter 2.

39. The answer is **A.** Rubber is the best material to reduce ESD problems. For more on this subject, see the "Protecting Equipment from Electrostatic Discharge" section in Chapter 2.

40. The answer is **B.** ESD is at its highest potential during low humidity atmospheric conditions. For more on this subject, see the "Protecting Equipment from Electrostatic Discharge" section in Chapter 2.

41. The answer is **C.** C-rated fire extinguishers are used only for electrical fires. For more on this subject, see the "Identifying Special Servicing Concerns" section in Chapter 2.

42. The answer is **B.** A DIMM memory module contains 168 pins, whereas a SIMM contains either 30 pins or 72 pins. For more on this subject, see the "Understanding Main Memory Modules" section in Chapter 6.

43. The answer is **B.** A 4M × 32 SIMM has a 16MB capacity. To determine the module's memory capacity, divide the specified second term representing width by either eight (non-parity) bits or nine (parity) bits to convert it to bytes, then multiply the calculated number of bytes by the first number, which is the depth in MB. For more on this subject, see the "Calculating Memory Capacities" section in Chapter 6.

44. The answer is **B.** A *soft power switch* is used on ATX system boards to power-down the system over a timed period. For more on this subject, see the "Understanding System Boards" section in Chapter 4.

45. The answer is **D.** CMOS contains only hardware device configuration settings. For more on this subject, see the "Understanding the ROM BIOS Chip" section in Chapter 4.

46. The answer is **B.** Slot 1 is used with a Pentium II processor. For more on this subject, see the "Identifying CPU Sockets and Slots" section in Chapter 5.

47. The answer is **A.** Intel 486 processors require 5 volts with the exception of the 486DX4 processor, which requires 3.3 volts. For more on this subject, see the "Identifying CPU Sockets and Slots" section in Chapter 5.

48. The answer is **B.** The 686 (Pentium Pro) contains 256K and 512K L2 cache. For more on this subject, see Table 5-1, "Summary of Intel CPU Specifications and Features," in Chapter 5.

49. The answer is **D.** After a laser printer passes self-test, the next task should be to check the interface connections between the host computer and printer. For more on this subject, see Table 10-1, "Laser Printer Problems and Causes," in Chapter 10.

50. The answer is **A.** The thermal fuse (thermostat) is used to protect the fuser assembly from overheating. For more on this subject, see Table 10-1, "Laser Printer Problems and Causes," in Chapter 10.

51. The answer is **D.** A defective primary corona wire will usually cause a laser printer to print totally black pages. For more on this subject, see Table 10-3, "Dot Matrix Printer Problems and Causes," in Chapter 10.

52. The answer is **A.** An impact printer head thermostat is probably functioning properly if printing slows after heavy usage. For more on this subject, see Table 10-3, "Dot Matrix Printer Problems and Causes," in Chapter 10.

53. The answer is **B.** Paper packed too tightly causes several or more sheets to be pulled simultaneously from a laser printer tray. For more on this subject, see Table 10-1, "Laser Printer Problems and Causes," in Chapter 10.

54. The answer is **C.** Laser toner is not dangerous to humans, whereas high voltage and laser beams are extremely dangerous. For more on this subject, see the sections, "Protecting Service Personnel from Electrical Shock and Laser Beams" and "Identifying Special Servicing Concerns" in Chapter 2.

55. The answer is **A.** Type III PC-Card Slots can be used to install portable disk storage drives. For more on this subject, see the "Recognizing System Unit Case Features," section in Chapter 3.

56. The answer is **A.** A software enabler must be installed before a portable computer recognizes a PC-Card. For more on this subject, see the "Recognizing System Unit Case Features" section in Chapter 3.

57. The answer is **B.** Only a NiMH (Nickel Metal-Hydride) battery can be used to replace a NiCad battery. For more on this subject, see the "Recognizing System Unit Case Features" section in Chapter 3.

58. The answer is **A.** A primary advantage to an active matrix display is that it is brighter than passive matrix displays. For more on this subject, see the "Recognizing System Unit Case Features" section in Chapter 3.

59. The answer is **C.** Data moves in both directions simultaneously with a full-duplex communication system. For more on this subject, see the "Identifying Network Cables and Connectors" section in Chapter 11.

60. The answer is **B.** If a NIC is configured incorrectly, the computer will fail to access the network. For more on this subject, see the "Defining Ethernet Architecture" section in Chapter 11.

61. The answer is **D.** If an NIC has an EPROM configuration switch, PnP or jumpers are not required to configure the NIC. For more on this subject, see the "Defining Ethernet Architecture" section in Chapter 11.

62. The answer is **C.** The MAC method used by Ethernet to access a network is called CSMA/CD (Carrier Sense Multiple Access/Collision Detection). For more on this subject, see the "Defining Ethernet Architecture" section in Chapter 11.

63. The answer is **B.** The primary Windows network protocol is NetBEUI (NetBIOS Extended User Interface). For more on this subject, see the "Understanding Network Protocols" section in Chapter 11.

64. The answer is **B.** The best approach is to resolve the situation quickly with little customer expense or effort. For more on this subject, see the "Managing Conflicts" section in Chapter 12.

65. The answer is **C.** Again, the best policy is to resolve the conflict and keep the customer. For more on this subject, see the "Managing Conflicts" section in Chapter 12.

Appendix

CD-ROM Contents

The CD-ROM included with this book contains the following materials:

- Adobe Acrobat Reader
- An electronic version of this book, *A+ Certification Core Module Test Prep Kit,* in `.pdf` format
- BeachFront Quizzer exam simulation software

Installing and Using Items on the CD-ROM

The following sections describe each product and include detailed instructions for installation and use.

The Adobe Acrobat Reader Version of *A+ Certification Core Module Test Prep Kit*

Adobe's Acrobat Reader is a helpful program that will enable you to view the electronic version of this book in the same page format as the actual book.

To install and run Adobe's Acrobat Reader and view the electronic version of this book, follow these steps:

1. Start Windows Explorer (if you're using Windows 95/98) or Windows NT Explorer (if you're using Windows NT), and then open the `Acrobat Reader` folder on the CD-ROM.

2. In the `Acrobat Reader` folder, double-click `ar32e301.exe` and follow the instructions presented onscreen for installing Adobe Acrobat Reader.

3. To view the electronic version of this book after you have installed Adobe's Acrobat Reader, start Windows Explorer (if you're using Windows 95) or Windows NT Explorer (if you're using Windows NT), and then open the `Book` folder on the CD-ROM.

4. In the `Book` folder, double-click the chapter or appendix file you want to view.

BeachFront Quizzer

The version of BeachFront Quizzer software included on the CD gives you an opportunity to test your knowledge by taking simulated exams. The BeachFront Quizzer product has many valuable features, including:

- Study session
- Standard exam
- Adaptive exam
- New exam every time
- Historical analysis

If you want more simulation questions, you can purchase the full retail version of the BeachFront Quizzer software from BeachFront Quizzer. See the BeachFront Quizzer ad in the back of the book.

To install and run BeachFront Quizzer, follow these steps:

1. View the contents of the BeachFront folder

2. Execute *ExamName* .exe, whereas *ExamName* is the name of the exam you wish to practice.

3. Follow the directions for installation.

Note: The CD key for BeachFront Quizzer is: 231166807835.

Index

A

Accelerated Graphics Port (AGP), 79, 87, 192
acetone, 206
active listening, 277, 279
active matrix screens, 54-55
adapter cards
  installing and configuring, 193-196
  Network Interface Cards (NICs), 189
  overview, 187-188
  sound, 189
  video, 189, 211-213
Advanced Micro Devices (AMD), 104
Advanced Power Management (ADM), 55
Advanced Technology X (ATX), 10
  power supplies, 13, 14
  system boards, 79-80, 92
  system unit case and, 53, 57
anti-static wrist strap, 32, 34
Application layer, OSI, 262
AT command set, 15, 214-215
ATAPI, 164
ATX. *See* Advanced Technology X

B

Baby AT system board , 81-83
Basic Input/Output System (BIOS), 11, 127-128
  error codes, 38
  keyboards and, 205
  ROM BIOS chip, 88
  SCSI IDs, 66
batteries, 55
baud rate, modem, 214
Bayonet Naur Connector (BNC), 15, 64, 190, 258
BEDO RAM, 129
body language, 278
Bootstrap Loader program, 90
bridges, 260
buffer memory, 162
Burst EDO (BEDO) RAM, 129
bus architectures, 84-88
  Accelerated Graphics Port (AGP), 87, 192
  block diagram example, 85
  categories, 84
  definition, 84
  Extended Industry Standard Architecture (EISA) , 85,191
  Industry Standard Architecture (ISA), 85,191
  PC Card, 87

continued

E

F

G

H

continued

K

L

M

N

O

ohmmeter, 36
onboard cache, hard disk, 162
open architecture, 7
Open System Interconnection (OSI)
    model, 262-263
overview, 189

P

parallel ports
    characteristics, 61
    Centronix interface, 237
    connector, 59, 61
    error codes, 38
    I/O addresses, 61-62, 185
    IRQ default settings, 61-62, 182
parity errors, 139, 137-138
Partition Magic, 156, 157
partitioning hard disk drives, 156
passive matrix screens, 54-55
PC Cards
    bus architecture, 87
    characteristics, 56
    classification of, 55-56
    dongles, 56
    replacement, 55
peer-to-peer LANs, 248
Pentium processors. *See* Intel proces-
    sors
performance of hard disk drive, 161-
    162

peripheral devices, 201-220
    exam material, 202
    keyboards, 205-206
    mice, 207-208
    modems, 213-216
    monitors, 209-211
    questions, 203-204, 217-220
    video adapter cards, 211-213
Peripheral-Component Interconnect
    (PCI) slot, 65, 86, 192
Personal Computer Memory Card
    International Association
    (PCMIA) cards. *See* PC Cards
physical formatting, 153-154
Physical layer, OSI, 262
pin grid array (PGA) package, 103,
    104, 114
PIO (Programmed Input/Output),
    164
planar board. *See* system board
platters, disc drive, 12, 159
platters, disk, 159
Plug-and-Play (PnP)
    BIOS and, 195
    PCI bus and, 192, 86
    ROM BIOS, 89
portable computer cases, 54-56
Power supplies
    overview, 13-14
    safety and, 28-29
    voltages, 14
power-on self test (POST)
    ROM BIOS chip, 127
    ROM BIOS chip and, 88-90
power-on self-test (POST), 11-12
    error codes, 38
    keyboard detection, 206
Power_Good signal , 13-14
Presentation layer, OSI, 262
primary corona wire, 229
printed circuit boards (PBCs).
    See circuit boards

R

S

continued

T

U

V

W

Z

IDG Books Worldwide, Inc. End-User License Agreement

READ THIS. You should carefully read these terms and conditions before opening the software packet(s) included with this book ("Book"). This is a license agreement ("Agreement") between you and IDG Books Worldwide, Inc. ("IDGB"). By opening the accompanying software packet(s), you acknowledge that you have read and accept the following terms and conditions. If you do not agree and do not want to be bound by such terms and conditions, promptly return the Book and the unopened software packet(s) to the place you obtained them for a full refund.

1. **License Grant.** IDGB grants to you (either an individual or entity) a nonexclusive license to use one copy of the enclosed software program(s) (collectively, the "Software") solely for your own personal or business purposes on a single computer (whether a standard computer or a workstation component of a multiuser network). The Software is in use on a computer when it is loaded into temporary memory (RAM) or installed into permanent memory (hard disk, CD-ROM, or other storage device). IDGB reserves all rights not expressly granted herein.

2. **Ownership.** IDGB is the owner of all right, title, and interest, including copyright, in and to the compilation of the Software recorded on the disk(s) or CD-ROM ("Software Media"). Copyright to the individual programs recorded on the Software Media is owned by the author or other authorized copyright owner of each program. Ownership of the Software and all proprietary rights relating thereto remain with IDGB and its licensers.

3. **Restrictions On Use and Transfer.**

   (a) You may only (i) make one copy of the Software for backup or archival purposes, or (ii) transfer the Software to a single hard disk, provided that you keep the original for backup or archival purposes. You may not (i) rent or lease the Software, (ii) copy or reproduce the Software through a LAN or other network system or through any computer subscriber system or bulletin-board system, or (iii) modify, adapt, or create derivative works based on the Software.

(b) You may not reverse engineer, decompile, or disassemble the Software. You may transfer the Software and user documentation on a permanent basis, provided that the transferee agrees to accept the terms and conditions of this Agreement and you retain no copies. If the Software is an update or has been updated, any transfer must include the most recent update and all prior versions.

4. **Restrictions on Use of Individual Programs.** You must follow the individual requirements and restrictions detailed for each individual program in the appendix of this Book. These limitations are also contained in the individual license agreements recorded on the Software Media. These limitations may include a requirement that after using the program for a specified period of time, the user must pay a registration fee or discontinue use. By opening the Software packet(s), you will be agreeing to abide by the licenses and restrictions for these individual programs that are detailed in the appendix and on the Software Media. None of the material on this Software Media or listed in this Book may ever be redistributed, in original or modified form, for commercial purposes.

5. **Limited Warranty.**

   (a) IDGB warrants that the Software and Software Media are free from defects in materials and workmanship under normal use for a period of sixty (60) days from the date of purchase of this Book. If IDGB receives notification within the warranty period of defects in materials or workmanship, IDGB will replace the defective Software Media.

   (b) IDGB AND THE AUTHOR OF THE BOOK DISCLAIM ALL OTHER WARRANTIES, EXPRESS OR IMPLIED, INCLUDING WITHOUT LIMITATION IMPLIED WARRANTIES OF MERCHANTABILITY AND FITNESS FOR A PARTICULAR PURPOSE, WITH RESPECT TO THE SOFTWARE, THE PROGRAMS, THE SOURCE CODE CONTAINED THEREIN, AND/OR THE TECHNIQUES DESCRIBED IN THIS BOOK. IDGB DOES NOT WARRANT THAT THE FUNCTIONS CONTAINED IN THE SOFTWARE WILL MEET YOUR REQUIREMENTS OR THAT THE OPERATION OF THE SOFTWARE WILL BE ERROR FREE.

(c) This limited warranty gives you specific legal rights, and you may have other rights that vary from jurisdiction to jurisdiction.

6. **Remedies.**

   (a) IDGB's entire liability and your exclusive remedy for defects in materials and workmanship shall be limited to replacement of the Software Media, which may be returned to IDGB with a copy of your receipt at the following address: Software Media Fulfillment Department, Attn.: *A+ Certification Core Module Test Prep Kit*, IDG Books Worldwide, Inc., 7260 Shadeland Station, Ste. 100, Indianapolis, IN 46256, or call 1-800-762-2974. Please allow three to four weeks for delivery. This Limited Warranty is void if failure of the Software Media has resulted from accident, abuse, or misapplication. Any replacement Software Media will be warranted for the remainder of the original warranty period or thirty (30) days, whichever is longer.

   (b) In no event shall IDGB or the author be liable for any damages whatsoever (including without limitation damages for loss of business profits, business interruption, loss of business information, or any other pecuniary loss) arising from the use of or inability to use the Book or the Software, even if IDGB has been advised of the possibility of such damages.

   (c) Because some jurisdictions do not allow the exclusion or limitation of liability for consequential or incidental damages, the above limitation or exclusion may not apply to you.

7. **U.S. Government Restricted Rights.** Use, duplication, or disclosure of the Software by the U.S. Government is subject to restrictions stated in paragraph (c)(1)(ii) of the Rights in Technical Data and Computer Software clause of DFARS 252.227-7013, and in subparagraphs (a) through (d) of the Commercial Computer — Restricted Rights clause at FAR 52.227-19, and in similar clauses in the NASA FAR supplement, when applicable.

8. **General.** This Agreement constitutes the entire understanding of the parties and revokes and supersedes all prior agreements, oral or written, between them and may not be modified or amended except in a writing signed by both parties hereto that specifically refers to this Agreement. This Agreement shall take precedence over any other documents that may be in conflict herewith. If any one or more provisions contained in this Agreement are held by any court or tribunal to be invalid, illegal, or otherwise unenforceable, each and every other provision shall remain in full force and effect.

my2cents.idgbooks.com

Installation Instructions

Each software item on the *A+ Certification Core Module Test Prep Kit*
CD-ROM is located in its own folder. To install a particular piece of software, open its folder with My Computer or Internet Explorer and follow
the installation instructions listed in the CD readme for that software.

For a listing of the software on the CD-ROM, please see the appendix.